The Greening of Economic Policy Reform
Volume I: Principles

Jeremy Warford
Mohan Munasinghe
Wilfrido Cruz

The World Bank
Washington, D.C.

Environment Papers are published to communicate the latest results of the Bank's environmental work to the development community with the least possible delay. The typescript of this paper therefore has not been prepared in accordance with the procedures appropriate to formal printed texts, and the World Bank accepts no responsibility for errors. Some sources cited in this paper may be informal documents that are not readily available.

Related World Bank publications include *Economywide Policies and the Environment* by Mohan Munasinghe and Wilfrido Cruz (World Bank Environment Paper No. 10) and *Environmental Impacts of Macroeconomic and Sectoral Policies* (forthcoming) edited by Mohan Munasinghe.

Library of Congress Cataloging-in-Publication Data

Warford, Jeremy J.
      The greening of economic policy reform / Jeremy Warford, Mohan
   Munasinghe, Wilford Cruz.
            p.   cm.
      Includes bibliographical references.
      Contents: v. 1 Principles—v. 2. Case studies
      ISBN 0-8213-3477-8
      1. Sustainable development—Case studies. 2. Economic policy—
   Case studies. 3. World Bank   I. Munasinghe, Mohan, 1945–   .
   II. Cruz, Wilfredo.   III. World Bank.   IV. Title.
   HC79.E5W36   1997
   333.7—dc20   95-39068
                                                              CIP

CONTENTS

VOLUME I

Foreword v

Acknowledgments vii

Authors viii

1. Overview 1

2. Explicit Environmental Incentives 9

3. Sectoral Policies 25

4. Macroeconomic Policy and the Adjustment Process 45

5. Linkages Between the Environment and Economywide Policies:
   Recent World Bank Experience 65

6. Case Study Summaries 81

7. Policy Implications 93

Bibliography 109

Abbreviations and Acronyms 119

Tables

4-1. Critical Environmental Links for Economic Planners 63
4-2. Critical Economic Policy Links for Environmental Planners 64
6-1: Scope of Economywide Policy-Environment Linkages Discussed
in Case Studies 92
7-1: Simple Example Action Impact Matrix (AIM) 101
7-2: Example of Environmental Issues: Matrix Indicators and Causes
of Selected Environmental Problems in Sri Lanka 102
7-3: Current Economic Conditions and Proposed Reforms in Sri Lanka . 104
7-4: Sri Lanka Action Impact Matrix 106

Figures

2-1: External Costs and Optimal Pollution 23
2-2: An Environmental Tax 23
2-3: Subsidizing Pollution 24
3-1: Marginal Opportunity Cost Pricing 44
3-2: Marginal Costs and Benefits of Reducing CO_2 Emissions 44

Boxes

3-1: Increasing Water Scarcity 29
3-2: Measuring Resource Use—the Metering Problem 31
4-1: Environmental Accounting 47
4-2: Poverty and the Environment 55
4-3: Environmental Concerns and Adjustment Lending 59
5-1: Fiscal Policy and Air Pollution in Mexico 70
5-2: Economic Transition and Sustainable Agriculture in China 74
5-3. Industrial Growth and Pollution in Indonesia 76

FOREWORD

Recent years have seen a wide range of economywide policy reform programs which have been undertaken in developing countries to address macroeconomic problems, such as those affecting international trade, government budgets, private investment, wages, and income distribution. Reform programs also address broad sectoral issues, such as those relating to agricultural productivity, industrial protection, and energy use. The economywide mechanisms for attaining these goals include altering the rates of exchange or interest, reducing government budgets, promoting market liberalization, fostering international openness, enhancing the role of the private sector, and strengthening government and market institutions—often coupled with pricing and other reforms in key sectors such as industry, agriculture, and energy.

Although these policies are typically not directed explicitly toward influencing the quality of the natural environment, they may, nonetheless have major impacts upon it, either positive or negative. This book (and its companion volume of case studies) shows that there are significant payoffs in attempting to understand such impacts better and to act upon them. Positive impacts of economywide reforms on the environment can be used to build constituencies for reform. Potential negative impacts need to be analyzed, monitored, and mitigated.

The importance of addressing economywide reforms and environmental management in an integrated manner has received growing recognition. As noted in the Bank's Annual Report on the environment, most country assistance strategies (CAS) now address the environmental challenges facing each country (World Bank, 1995, *Mainstreaming the Environment*). The CAS is the principal statement of the World Bank's overall development strategy in a given country. In some country assistance strategies, the links between environmental problems and their underlying causes are discussed (e.g., natural resource or energy price distortions). In others, the focus is on government efforts to address environmental issues at the country level. Recent examples include the CAS for Chile, China, Hungary, Latvia, Niger, Senegal, Swaziland, and Thailand. For example, in Senegal, although the main focus is on stimulating economic growth, the environment is listed as one of five problem areas that need specific attention.

Environmental considerations are also featured in CAS discussions of sectoral policies and lending programs. These include water resource management (e.g., Brazil, India, FYR Macedonia, and Peru), urban sanitation (most countries), energy efficiency (China, and various countries in Eastern and Central Europe), industrial pollution control (Brazil, China, Ghana, and Thailand), mining (Estonia, Ghana, Peru, and Poland, among others), and agriculture (especially countries in Africa and Latin America) (World Bank, 1995, *Mainstreaming the Environment*).

Although much literature of a theoretical nature on this topic is emerging, there has until recently been little empirical work to help improve our understanding of the links between economywide policies and the environment. In some instances, the direction of environmental impacts stemming from economywide policy reform is fairly straightforward. The extent of the impact, however, invariably requires empirical analysis. In more complex cases, even the direction of the impact is ambiguous. In view of their location-specific nature, involving a range of economic, physical, institutional, and cultural variables, there is a clear need for more case study material to enhance our understanding of these relationships.

The case studies summarized here (and presented in full in Volume II), which have been carried out within the World Bank over the last several years, are a contribution to this objective. They have already provided the basis for a comprehensive paper on economywide policies and the environment that was approved by the Bank's Board of Executive Directors, and presented at a special session of the 50th Anniversary Annual Meetings of the World Bank and International Monetary Fund in Madrid, October 1994 (World Bank, 1994, *Economywide Policies and the Environment: Emerging Lessons from Experience*). The case studies reflect a wide range of country situations and environmental problems. Pollution issues are addressed with reference to air quality and energy use in Poland and Sri Lanka, while a variety of natural resource-related issues are covered in the other studies: deforestation and land degradation in Costa Rica, migration and deforestation in the Philippines, degradation of agricultural lands due to overgrazing in Tunisia, fertility losses due to extension of cultivated areas in Ghana, water resource depletion in Morocco, and wildlife management in Zimbabwe.

The case studies also utilize a variety of analytical methods to illustrate the different approaches available for identifying the environmental implications of economywide reforms. These methods range from those tracing the links between economic incentives and resource use through direct observation, to others relying on more complex economic modeling of policies and their environmental effects. In all the studies, however, the analytical approach uniformly requires identifying key environmental concerns and relating these to the agenda of priority sectoral and macroeconomic reforms under consideration. The analysis underscores the formidable difficulties of developing a general methodology to trace all possible environmental impacts of a package of adjustment reforms. At the same time, it offers evidence that careful case-specific empirical work may help identify better ways to deal with potentially serious impacts of specific economywide policies on high-priority environmental problems. We obviously have a long way to go before environmental impact assessment of economic policies can be used systematically in public decisionmaking; nevertheless, this work helps to reinforce the case that imperfect knowledge should not be an excuse for inaction. In many important cases, the potential environmental consequences of economic policies may be discernible, and the direction in which compensatory or defensive measures should go, is quite apparent.

Andrew Steer
Director
Environment Department

Vinod Thomas
Director
Economic Development Institute

The World Bank
Washington, D.C.

ACKNOWLEDGMENTS

We acknowledge the comments and suggestions that were received during the course of many discussions, workshops, and reviews, from colleagues within and outside the World Bank. These include Richard Ackermann, Dennis Anderson, Maria Concepcion J. Cruz, Luis Constantino, Partha Dasgupta, Mohamed El-Ashry, Ved Gandhi, Christopher Gibbs, Gunnar Eskeland, Stein Hansen, T. J. Ho, William Hyde, Emmanuel Jimenez, Ronald MacMorran, Karl-Göran Mäler, Paul Martin, David Pearce, Jorn Rattsoe, Robert Repetto, Iona Sebastian, Robert Schneider, Anand Seth, Hu Tao, Adriaan Ten-Kate, Laura Tuck, Hirofumi Uzawa, and David Wheeler. We have attempted to address all their comments and are solely responsible for any remaining inadequacies.

We are especially grateful to our case study authors: Gregory Amacher, Robin Bates, Jan Bojö, Robert Cunliffe, Boguslaw Fiodor, Herminia Francisco, Ian Goldin, Shreekant Gupta, Ramon Lopez, Paul Martin, Peter Meier, Stephen D. Mink, Kay Muir-Leresche, Zeinab Partow, Annika Persson, David Roland-Host, and Tilak Siyambalapitiya.

Publication of this book was sponsored by the Environment Department and the Economic Development Institute of the World Bank. We thank Mohamed T. El-Ashry, Andrew Steer, Vinod Thomas, and Hatsuya Azumi for their support.

This book has also benefitted greatly from comments received when a condensed version was presented to the Board of Executive Directors of the World Bank, as well as at a special Environment Seminar convened at the Fiftieth Anniversary Annual Meetings of the World Bank and the International Monetary Fund in Madrid.

The complex research program behind this book was made manageable by the excellent Economywide Policies and Environment project team. We especially thank Adelaida Schwab, Noreen Beg, Shreekant Gupta, Annika Persson, and Nalin Kishor. Karen Danczyk assisted with the editorial work; Luz Rivera and Daisy Martinez provided secretarial support. Jay Dougherty and Rebecca Kary of Alpha-Omega Services, Inc., provided editorial and layout services.

The project was supported in part by generous contributions from the governments of Norway and Sweden.

Jeremy J. Warford, Mohan Munasinghe, and Wilfrido Cruz

AUTHORS

Jeremy J. Warford is Visiting Professor of Environmental Economics, Centre for Social and Economic Research on the Global Environment, University College, London. He was formerly Senior Adviser in the Environment Department and Economic Development Institute, the World Bank.

Mohan Munasinghe is Distinguished Visiting Professor of Environmental Management, University of Colombo, Sri Lanka. He is on leave from the World Bank, where he was Chief of the Pollution and Environmental Economics Division, Environment Department.

Wilfrido Cruz is Environmental Economist at the Environment and Natural Resources Division of the Economic Development Institute of the World Bank. He was formerly Economist at the World Resources Institute, a leading environmental policy research organization.

1

Overview

ENVIRONMENTAL DEGRADATION poses an increasing threat to economic growth and development prospects worldwide. The range of issues categorized as "environmental" is, of course, huge. It includes deforestation, elimination of species, soil erosion, pesticide buildup, industrial and municipal pollution, acid rain, climate change, and the threat to the ozone layer.

Developing countries are in a specially difficult position. Unlike the industrial countries, most of them still have to resolve massive local environmental problems such as the provision of safe drinking water and sanitation services, their difficulties being compounded with regard both to the degradation of agricultural and forest resources, as well as the need for urban services by explosive rates of population growth.At the same time they are confronted with the global problems arising from the emission of transboundary pollutants, which, at least to date, are primarily due to economic growth in the industrial world.

Attitudes toward environmental matters in developing countries have changed significantly over the past two decades. At the time of the 1972 Stockholm Conference on the environment, there was a fairly clear north-south split on the issue. The developing countries generally regarded environmental concerns as a luxury that only the rich nations could afford, and they resented the efforts of interest groups in the industrial countries to persuade them otherwise. Since then, there has been a considerable narrowing of the gap between north and south. This is the good news. The bad news is, of course, that a major reason for the change is that in the intervening period environmental degradation has become so serious that its implications for economic growth are becoming increasingly obvious.

Indeed, far from being a luxury, there is increasing evidence that sound environmental management is essential if economic growth is to be achieved—even in the short run. This, however, is not to say that the developing countries and the industrial countries see eye to eye on all the issues, and marked differences continued to be observed at the 1992 United Nations Conference on Environment and Development. For example, the former, quite correctly, point to the latter's responsibility for the state of the global environment, and claim that it is unfair to expect them to invest heavily in measures to redress the situation. On the other hand, the growth in energy consumption in the developing world in the future will considerably outstrip that of the presently industrial countries. Their contribution to incremental atmospheric pollution and climate issues is thus a legitimate concern.

Traditionally the main focus of environmental economics has been on micro-level resource allocation (cost-benefit and cost-effectiveness analysis combined with environmental impact assessment of individual projects), with latterly increasing emphasis on questions of financing and resource mobilization. While these concerns remain of importance, and indeed, warrant still further effort, it is becoming increasingly evident that they are not sufficient to make a serious dent in the main environmental problems facing the planet, and that it is necessary to devote more effort to using economics to integrate environmental issues into the mainstream of economic policymaking. This involves, *inter alia*, ongoing review of the prospects for so-called sustainable development, which calls into question commonly held views about the role of technical progress, human capacity to adapt to natural resource scarcity, and the potential for substituting manmade for natural capital.

A switch in emphasis from micro to sectoral or macro concerns, is therefore under way. The growing physical interdependence between nations, and importance of the "global commons" opens up still further avenues where economic policy formulation has a potentially major role to play. Research needs, however, abound. These include valuation issues as well as analysis of the conceptual and practical problems involved in integrating environmental management into economic policymaking. In general, the main need appears to be to recognize the essentially multidisciplinary nature of environmental issues, and to improve understanding of the linkages between economic policies and the natural world. Economic research needs are primarily of an applied nature: it may indeed be argued that there is no "environmental economics" as such—merely the application of well established theoretical principles in a wider context. Existing tools are highly relevant, but extending the horizons of economists—over space and time—is still required.

Policy and Project Interventions

It is increasingly being recognized that most environmental problems are less the result of individual large scale development projects that have gone wrong than the combined consequences of countless relatively small scale activities—unsustainable agricultural practices, small scale polluting activities, and individual decisions to exploit tropical forest resources. Subjecting each such decision to social cost-benefit analysis, environmental impact assessment, or regulation, or indeed a system of environmental taxes that requires monitoring of individual actions, is often not feasible. It is therefore necessary to search for the underlying causes of such activities, and identify policy interventions (which will often have to be somewhat blunt instruments) aimed at the source, rather than the symptom of the problems.[1]

Because of the pervasive nature of environmental problems, the traditional project-by-project approach, while important and deserving of more effort, therefore needs to be supplemented by the integration of environmental management into economic policymaking at all levels of government. Special attention should be given to the role of economic incentives in influencing environmental behavior, and existing economic policies should be subjected to environmental evaluation. Policies with a wide ranging impact—i.e., those of a sectoral or macro-economic nature—are specially relevant. Many of them may have a profound impact—for good or ill—on the environment.[2] Fiscal, exchange rate, agriculture, energy, industrial, and land tenure policies might all be expected to have major environmental

implications, but in practice environmental consequences have traditionally not been considered in their formulation.

For an individual country, an environmental action program should therefore consist of the following three deceptively simple steps:

(a) identification of major environmental problems in a country, assisted where possible by cost-benefit analysis and efforts to relate damage to national income accounts

(b) search for proximate and underlying causes of damage

(c) on the basis of the previous step, identify policy reforms and investments, and sources of funding.

The second of these steps is at the heart of the analysis. Proximate causes are relatively easy to identify. Much more difficult, but of primary importance, is the analysis of underlying causes. Typically these will be found in economic incentives, often combined with a complex mix of social and political factors. For example, it may be easy to identify the inefficient productive processes of certain industrial enterprises as being the source of air pollution. It is, however, more difficult to understand the forces that bring this about, and to determine the policy reforms that will not simply affect individual plants, but have pervasive effects, impacting on a wide variety of industrial operations.

There are in practice many opportunities for economic policy reforms which also yield environmental benefits. Environmental degradation often stems from market distortions, which may be explained by externalities or "commons" problems, or which are induced by government policies. The search for policy reforms which address market failure and also improve the environment

---

[1]This theme was elaborated on in World Bank 1987. A similar message emerges from the Brundtland Report (WCED 1987).

[2]A similar argument may be applied to health, which may be impacted directly, through income effects, or indirectly, through changes in the natural environment resulting from macro- or sector-level policies. See Warford 1995. For a review of the literature, see Cooper-Weil et al. 1990.

(i.e., "win-win" actions) should be a central feature of a country's environmental policy.[3]

Generally, the range of technical options that might be employed to address environmental problems is also well known, but practice clearly lags well behind theory. This gives rise to the question as to why technically and economically efficient solutions are not in fact adopted. This is an area where economics should play an even more important role, namely the analysis of underlying causes of environmental problems. In many cases, the root cause may lie in policies or events that are at first sight far removed from the environmental problem itself. Environmental damage may, of course, stem not only from incorrect government actions (sins of commission), but also of failure to take action to reduce environmental degradation act (sins of omission). Either way, improved understanding of underlying causes is a prerequisite for policy reform.

Structure of the Volumes

This is the first of two volumes that address the relationships between economywide policies and the environment, with special reference to recent World Bank research efforts.

Volume I contains seven chapters. After this Overview, Chapter 2, Explicit Environmental Incentives, briefly reviews economic and other policies specifically designed to address environmental problems, and which are essentially required to address the consequences of market failure. The chapter discusses the role of market-based instruments and regulatory approaches to environmental management and, in light of experience from the industrial countries, the feasibility and relevance of such approaches in the developing world.

Chapter 3, Sectoral Policies, contains a review of the relationships between sectoral policies pertaining, for example, to agriculture, energy, and industry, and the often unanticipated but major environmental consequences stemming from them. Emphasis is given to the scope for achieving "win-win" reforms, i.e., those that satisfy both economic and environmental objectives.

Chapter 4, Macroeconomic Policy and the Adjustment Process, then addresses the general nature of the linkages between macroeconomic and sectoral policies and the environment. It introduces the generic findings resulting from the series of case studies conducted by the World Bank, and also draws upon the lessons from work done by other researchers in recent years. The results of the various studies are discussed in terms of various themes, namely (a) efficiency-motivated policies (b) policy, market and institutional imperfections (c) macroeconomic stability and (d) longer-term poverty and income distributional effects.

Following this introduction to the case studies in terms of the themes that emerge from them, Chapter 6, Case Study Summaries, briefly introduces the research on a country-by-country basis. Clearly, many of the issues identified in the preceding chapter interact with each other in any real-world situation, as illustrated in this chapter. In general, the studies provide convincing evidence of the environmental impact of countrywide policies, and for the conclusion that the adjustment process is both a necessary, but not sufficient condition, for long-term, sustainable, growth.

Chapter 7, Policy Implications, draws together the conclusions of the case studies, and makes recommendations about the integration of environmental concerns into economic decisionmaking. It also proposes as a tool of analysis, the *Action Impact Matrix*, which can be used to highlight relationships and mesh economic decisions with priority environmental and social im-

---

[3]The scope for "win-win" policies is heavily emphasized in WCED 1987 and in World Bank 1992k.

pacts. Chapter 7 concludes Volume I, which, as it contains the essence of the case study results, can be read as a self-contained document. For the reader interested in a more detailed treatment of the case studies, this is to be found in Volume II.[4]

Scope of the Study

Economywide policies are defined here to include all policies of a pervasive nature. Although the emphasis of the book is upon economic policies (such as energy and agriculture sector pricing, trade and fiscal policies, and privatization), other sectoral policies (including the legal and institutional framework, land tenure arrangements, population, and social policies and attitudes) are all relevant. Indeed, understanding of the interplay between these various factors is essential if economic policy prescriptions are to be firmly based.

A wide range of economywide policy reform programs has been undertaken to address macroeconomic problems (such as those affecting international trade, government budgets, private investment, wages, and income distribution) and broad sectoral issues (such as those relating to agricultural productivity, industrial protection, and energy use). The economywide mechanisms for attaining these goals include: altering the rates of exchange or interest, reducing government budget deficits, promoting market liberalization, fostering international openness, enhancing the role of the private sector, and strengthening government and market institutions, often coupled with pricing and other reforms in key sectors such as industry, agriculture and energy.

Although these policies are not directed explicitly towards influencing the quality of the natural environment, they may, nonethe-

less, affect it for good or ill. This book indicates that there are significant benefits to be gained from a better understanding of such linkages. Focusing attention on the positive impacts of economywide reforms on the economy as well as the environment, helps to build consensus for such reforms and improves cooperation among both environmental and economic managers. No less important are the potential negative environmental impacts of economywide policies that need to be analyzed, monitored and mitigated.

In some instances the *direction* of environmental impact stemming from economywide policy reform is fairly straightforward. The *extent* of the impact, however, invariably requires empirical analysis. In more complex cases, even the direction of the impact is ambiguous. Therefore, the book relies heavily on empirical findings and draws on a country-specific approach to deal with links between economywide policies and the environment.

The book contains a review of World Bank case studies and other recent research, and provides examples that reflect a wide range of country situations and environmental problems. Pollution issues are addressed with reference to air quality and industrial pollution in Poland. Environmental aspects of energy use are addressed in the Sri Lanka case. A variety of natural resource related issues are covered in the other studies: deforestation and land degradation in Costa Rica; migration and deforestation in the Philippines; degradation of agricultural lands due to overgrazing in Tunisia; fertility losses due to extension of cultivated areas in Ghana; water resource depletion in Morocco; and wildlife management in Zimbabwe.

The case studies also utilize a variety of analytical methods to illustrate the different approaches available for identifying the environmental implications of economywide reforms. The methods range from those

---

[4]W. Cruz, M. Munasinghe, and J. Warford (eds.), *The Greening of Economic Policy Reform, Volume II, Case Studies* (Washington, D.C.: World Bank).

tracing the links between economic incentives and resource use through direct observation, to others relying on more complex economic modeling of policies and their environmental effects. In all the studies, however, the analytical approach requires identifying key environmental concerns and relating these to the agenda of priority sectoral and macroeconomic reforms under consideration.

The analysis underscores the difficulties of developing a general methodology to trace environmental impacts of policy reform. At the same time, it offers evidence that careful case-specific empirical work on the most important potential environmental impacts may help identify better ways to deal with them, and sets out several practical steps by which the findings may be implemented in operational work. The book also demonstrates the considerable scope for developing better analytical tools to trace environment-economic policy linkages.

Main Findings and Conclusions

The specific findings of this study are presented below—grouped according to the principal ways in which economywide policies interact with the environment, and highlighting how they might help in the design of better adjustment programs.

- Removal of price distortions, promotion of market incentives, and relaxation of other constraints (which are among the main features of adjustment-related reforms), generally will contribute to both economic and environmental gains. For example, reforms which improve the efficiency of industrial or energy related activities could reduce both economic waste and environmental pollution. Similarly, improving land tenure rights and access to financial and social services not only yields economic gains but also promotes better environmental stewardship.

- Unintended adverse side effects occur, however, when economywide reforms are undertaken while other neglected policy, market or institutional imperfections persist. The remedy does not generally require reversal of the original economywide reforms, but rather the implementation of additional complementary measures (both economic and noneconomic) that remove such policy, market and institutional difficulties. Such complementary measures are not only generally environmentally beneficial in their own right, but also help to broaden the effectiveness of economywide reforms. Typical examples of potential environmental damage caused by remaining imperfections include:

Policy distortions: Export promotion and trade liberalization, that increase the export profitability of a natural resource, might encourage excessive extraction or harvesting of this resource if it were underpriced or subsidized (for example, low stumpage fees for timber).

Market failures: Economic expansion induced by successful adjustment may be associated with excessive environmental damage, for example, if external environmental effects of economic activities (such as pollution), are not adequately reflected in market prices.

Institutional constraints: The environmental and economic benefits of economywide reforms could be negated by unaddressed institutional issues, such as poor accountability of state-owned enterprises, inadequately defined property rights, or weak financial intermediation—which tend to undermine incentives for sustainable resource management.

• Measures aimed at restoring macroeconomic stability will generally yield environmental benefits, since instability undermines sustainable resource use. For example, stability encourages a longer-term view on the part of decisionmakers at all levels, and lower inflation rates lead to clearer pricing signals and better investment decisions by economic agents. These are essential prerequisites for encouraging environmentally sustainable activities.

• The stabilization process also may have unforeseen adverse short-term impacts on the environment. For example, while general reductions in government spending are deemed appropriate, targeting these cutbacks would be desirable to avoid disproportionate penalties on environmental protection measures. Another important issue is the possible short-term impact of adjustment on poverty and unemployment, which may aggravate existing pressures on fragile and "open access" natural resources by the poor, due to the lack of economic opportunities. In this case, appropriate measures designed to address the possible adverse social consequences of adjustment will be justified even further—on environmental grounds.

• Economywide policies will have additional longer-term effects on the environment through employment and income distribution changes. Several of the examples confirm one predictable conclusion—adjustment-induced changes generate new economic opportunities and sources of livelihood, thereby alleviating poverty and reducing pressures on the environment due to overexploitation of fragile resources by the unemployed. However, while growth is an essential element of sustainable development, it will necessarily increase pressures on environmental resources. Increasing efficiency and reducing waste, as well as properly valuing resources, will help reshape the structure of growth and reduce undesirable environmental impacts.

Practical Implications

The findings have important policy implications. While the relationships between economywide policies and the environment are complex, there is usually a small number of identifiable linkages affecting high priority environmental concerns. The environmental analysis and implementation efforts related to specific programs can therefore be sufficiently focused to be practical and effective. Proper recognition of the generally positive environmental consequences of economywide policy reforms would help to build additional support for such programs. At the same time, broader recognition of the underlying economic and policy causes of environmental problems can enhance support for environmental initiatives—both in terms of environmental policies as well as projects. The following are immediate steps that can be taken by decisionmakers:

• *Problem Identification*: More systematic efforts are needed to monitor environmental trends and anticipate emerging problems when policy reform proposals are being prepared and implemented. A review of the range of currently available environmental information would help identify the highest priority pre-existing or emerging environmental problems, and their sensitivity to policy measures.

• *Analysis*: Serious potential environmental impacts of proposed economywide reforms identified in the problem identification stage should be carefully assessed, to the extent that data and resources permit. Many of the techniques and examples presented in this book will be helpful in tracing the simpler and more obvious links between economywide policies and the environment.

- *Remedies*: Where potential adverse impacts of economywide reforms can be identified and analyzed successfully, targeted complementary environmental policies or investments need to be implemented in order to mitigate environmental damage, and enhance beneficial effects. Where linkages are difficult to trace *ex ante*, greater reliance should be placed on preparing contingency plans to be invoked *ex post* (see below).

- *Follow-up*: A follow-up system for monitoring the impacts of economic reform programs on environmentally sensitive areas should be designed, and resources made available to address environmental problems that may arise during implementation.

2

Explicit Environmental Incentives

General Principles

IN RECENT YEARS A GOOD DEAL OF ANALYTICAL WORK has addressed the potential role of economic instruments in dealing with environmental problems, and this has been matched by a perceptible shift in actual policies, particularly in the industrial countries. Attention has focused to a considerable extent on pollution, but the general principles contained in the literature and recent policy experience are of wider application. Economic instruments may take a variety of forms, ranging from measures designed explicitly to achieve environmental objectives, such as pollution charges and taxes, tradeable permits and subsidies, as well as user charges for water resources, energy and transportation, where inefficient usage has adverse environmental consequences.

For further elaboration of the major themes contained in this chapter, see Pearce and Warford 1993, and Pearce and Turner 1990.

This chapter considers the role of economic instruments and policies with respect to their use for explicitly environmental purposes, central to the ongoing debate being the appropriate roles of market-based instruments versus "command-and-control" approaches to environmental management. The environmental consequences of sectoral policies will be considered in Chapter 3.

Traditionally, environmental economics has focused heavily upon the failure of markets to achieve an optimal allocation of resources, with externalities, and, to a lesser extent, public goods problems. An externality can be defined as any action which has an unintended impact upon another party's welfare, and which is uncompensated or unappropriated. The classic case may be represented by an industrial plant that discharges waste into a river, imposing downstream costs on fisheries, municipal water suppliers, or other industrial water users. As long as the damage done remains less than fully compensated, an external cost is said to exist. It should also be noted that an external benefit can be defined in a parallel way.

Figure 2–1 illustrates the concept of external cost. MB is the marginal benefit, or profit derived from producing an extra unit of the polluting product, or in other words, the polluter's "marginal net private benefit" curve. Typically, MB can be expected to decline as output expands. The marginal damage cost (MDC) represents the marginal cost of damage to those who suffer from the pollution. In the absence of any government intervention, the level of output of the polluting product will be at Q_1; i.e., output will increase up to the point that net marginal gains from further expansion are zero. However, Q_1 corresponds to a greater than optimal output; in fact, the optimum is at Q_2, where marginal benefits equal marginal costs. Beyond this point, marginal damage costs are greater than marginal benefits, while up to that point, the benefits of further output exceed the marginal damage costs.

This illustration introduces the concept of "optimal pollution." In practice, it is unrealistic, and indeed undesirable, to aim at elimination of pollution or most other types of environmental degradation. This in fact is of central importance for environmental policy, in which tradeoffs, or choices between environmental and other developmental objectives must continually be made.

It will be observed that most of the economics literature, and indeed practice, with regard to the use of explicit environmental incentives, has been in the context of pollution problems. This is not to say that environmental objectives have not played a part in the design of economic instruments employed in the agriculture or forestry sectors. For example, the use of stumpage fees aimed at reducing depletion of forest resources, or the use of tradeable permits for fisheries, could be defined as being primarily "environmental." There is no way of unambiguously defining such a policy as sectoral or environmental, and in organizing the material in this book we have tended to treat policies which have other than a purely environmental objective in the sectoral or macroeconomic policy category.

Explicit instruments may be defined to include charges and taxes (with an important distinction being made between emissions charges/taxes and product charges/taxes), subsidies, deposit-refund schemes and performance bonds, market creation and financial enforcement incentives. The general rationale for market-based instruments as opposed to regulatory methods has been extensively covered in the literature, with some aspects of special relevance to environmental health having recently been reviewed for the World Health Organization. In practice, economic and regulatory instruments tend to be used in combination with each other. In selecting the appropriate environmental policy instrument, the following criteria should be employed:

- Environmental effectiveness
- Economic efficiency (in terms of cost-benefit, or cost-effectiveness tests)
- Revenue raising
- Equity, fairness, acceptability
- Administrative feasibility and cost

It is possible that the optimum level of output, Q_2, in Figure 2–1 could be achieved by other means. In principle, the party or parties suffering from the externality (i.e., those to whom MDC applies) could ask the polluter what sum of money he would require to reduce his pollution load from the existing Q_1 level. In fact, reducing pollution to Q_2 could be in both parties' interests because while the damaged party should be willing to pay any amount less than MDC, the polluter should be willing to accept any amount greater than MB. Such a bargaining approach could therefore result in the optimal level, Q_2. Similarly, if the damaged party held the property rights to the whole area, the polluter could be permitted to pay for marginal damage caused. This would be both acceptable to the sufferer and to the polluter up to, but not beyond, the Q_2 level.

The foregoing suggests that in theory, and according to a narrow economic efficiency objective, if individuals can create markets in externalities, there is no need for governments to intervene, regardless of who owns the property rights.[1] In practice, this possibility faces a great many difficulties. First of all, it does not work when other than competitive conditions apply in the economy. Moreover, its apparent unfairness inhibits cooperation. Its distributional implications are unsatisfactory—for example, it could not be used to handle long-term issues in which the damaged parties are future generations since they have no bargaining power. (Existence of disproportionate bargaining power is also particularly relevant with regard to the resolution of global environmental prob-

lems such as the greenhouse effect.)

In fact a central obstacle to the successful outcome of a bargaining solution, and one which is of generic significance in the environmental debate, concerns the incidence of the costs and benefits of environmental improvement. Conflict of interest—or externalities—tends to characterize the environmental problem. Vested interests are important, and almost by definition the poor or disadvantaged suffer at the expense of those who have a greater say in the decisionmaking process. While there are some examples of the bargaining solution in practice, they are few and far between. When the parties damaged are politically weak, poorly organized, or unaware of their rights, or are simply future generations, there are reasons to be pessimistic about reliance upon the bargaining solution to resolving environmental problems.

Market-Based Instruments versus Command and Control

Where the market does not work properly, some form of public intervention is required. Assuming that the political will exists to overcome the distributional and political obstacles referred to above, essentially three different approaches can be employed: command and control, in which pollution or emissions standards are set and emitters are simply required to achieve those standards; environmental taxes, in which polluters are taxed according to the level of emissions produced; and a system of tradeable permits, in which polluters are allocated permits to pollute up to a given standard, but are given the option of buying and selling those permits in the market place.

Environmental taxes and tradeable permits are examples of market-based incentives. Command-and-control approaches, on the other hand, do not make use of the market at all. There is a considerable literature on this subject, with the work done by Allen

---

[1] See Coase 1960.

Kneese and his colleagues at Resources for the Future in the 1960s, and the Organisation for Economic Co-operation and Development (OECD) advocacy of the "Polluter Pays Principle" in the 1970s being of major significance.[2] In general, economists have tended to favor market-based instruments over command-and-control or regulatory ones, on the grounds that the former will allow pollution control targets to be attained more cheaply.[3]

The argument is that the command-and-control approach is deficient in a number of ways. First, it requires the regulator to use up resources to acquire information that polluters already possess. Second, polluters vary in the ease with which they can abate pollution. Their costs of control therefore differ, and control is not concentrated in the sources that find it cheapest to abate pollution. Overall, compliance with the standard are therefore not achieved as cheaply as they could be. Market-based instruments on the other hand may encourage pollution control efforts to be carried out where it is cheapest to do so.

Note, however, that command-and-control does have an important place in the array of environmental instruments, and any environmental policy should employ a judicious mix of economic incentives and regulations. In general the economists' argument is that the current dominance of command and control is an imbalance that needs to be corrected. They would, however, typically acknowledge that regulations have a role; for example outright bans, or specific means of treatment or disposal of certain toxic or hazardous wastes may be required.

---

[2]Kneese 1964 and OECD 1975. For a recent review of the literature, see Eskeland and Jimenez 1991.

[3]See Baumol and Oates 1988. Proof that marketable permits minimize compliance costs can be found in Pearce and Turner 1990, Chapter 8, and in Tietenberg 1985.

Second best issues (see below) might also indicate cautious adoption of market-based instruments. Furthermore, command-and-control measures tend to appeal because of the greater certainty of achieving given effluent or ambient standards; the experimentation that may be inherent in the use of market-based instruments may make reliance upon them less feasible.

Environmental Taxes

Market-based incentive systems operate by simulating market conditions. An environmental tax may alter the price of the polluting input or technology, or the polluting product, or all of them. From an efficiency standpoint, an ideal tax would be one which equals the MDC imposed by the discharge of a pollutant. This is depicted in Figure 2–2, the optimal discharge, as noted earlier, being at point Q_2. The effect of such a tax is to shift the after-tax MB curve down to MB(t). By leaving the firm to maximize its after-tax profits the firm automatically goes to Q_2.

The case for an environmental tax is largely based upon its cost-effectiveness in achieving a given environmental target. Emitters of CO_2, for example, can be charged according to the carbon content of the fuels they burn. Coal would attract a higher charge than oil which would attract a higher charge than natural gas. The effect of the tax would be to induce: (a) substitution of lower carbon fuels for high carbon fuels; (b) substitution of noncarbon energy (nuclear power, renewables) for carbon energy; and (c) energy conservation.

A carbon tax would be a relatively efficient means of achieving the environmental objective of reducing CO_2 emissions, since a fairly direct and unambiguous relationship between fuel consumption and emissions can be estimated. However, in many cases, taxes on inputs are somewhat blunt instruments, since they do not discriminate between more and less efficient users of the input. There may not, in other words, be a proportional relationship between consumption of the input, such as fuel, and the emission of pollutants. A tax on coal consumption, designed to reduce emissions of particulates, for example, would not in itself encourage environmentally sound behavior. Nor would a tax on electricity consumption at the retail level. A gasoline tax may also be an imperfect instrument, since proportionality between fuel consumption and emissions cannot be assumed. A pollution tax on outputs, or effluents, is a more precise instrument. Unfortunately, this option is often precluded by the cost of the sophisticated inspection and monitoring system that pollution taxes require.

A major advantage of environmental taxes, compared with tradeable permits or command-and-control alternatives, is of course that they raise revenue. In principle, such revenue could be used as a fiscally neutral substitute for other taxes. This raises the issue of "green taxes," discussed below.[4]

Tradeable Permits

Tradeable permits require an acceptable level of pollution to be determined. This may be expressed, for example, as an allowable national emissions level for SO_2. Permits are then issued for the level of pollutants up to the allowable level. Once the initial allocation is made (a significant distributional issue), polluters are free to trade pollution rights. This will permit reduction in SO_2 to be done most cheaply. A firm that finds it comparatively easy to abate pollution will find it profitable to sell its permits to a polluter who finds it expensive to abate. The overall environmental standard will remain unaltered because permits just sufficient to achieve the quality standard in aggregate have been issued. The reallocation of permits between polluters minimizes the

costs of compliance with the standard because it concentrates the costs of control on those who can most easily afford to adopt abatement measures.

A frequent objection to tradeable permits is an ethical one, namely that industries are given a "license to pollute," as long as they can afford to do so. However, all regulatory approaches allow pollution up to the level of the standard, and tradeable permits are no different. If the criticism is intended to mean that there should be zero pollution then this would have to be justified—as in the case of all other types of control—in terms of some nonefficiency objective.

Economic Instruments and Transboundary Effects

Greenhouse gases (GHGs)

A similar set of theoretical and practical issues arise when the analysis of market-based instruments for pollution control is extended from the national to the global level. For example, there have recently been strenuous efforts to arrive at a global protocol on greenhouse gases, which could include uniform targets for greenhouse gas reduction. But, just as it is inefficient to set the same target reduction in emissions for each polluter, it is equally inefficient to set each country the same target. While it may appear equitable for each country to achieve, say, a stable emissions target, the definition of fairness becomes ambiguous where the cost of achieving the target varies from country to country.

The aim of any measure to reduce greenhouse gas emissions should clearly be to bias the reductions towards those countries which can most easily achieve them. The logic of this requirement is fairly simple: if one country has lower costs of abatement than another, it will be cheaper to require more control in that country than in the high abatement cost country. A protocol which requires equal emissions reductions by

[4]Page 1977.

country offends this principle and hence incurs an unnecessary aggregate cost burden. Equally, any burden-sharing arrangement must allow for the development needs of the developing nations.

An internationally agreed upon set of standards for achieving GHG reduction could in principle achieve the minimum cost objective, particularly because global warming would affect different countries in different ways. A few may conceivably gain from climate change. But even if all lose, some will lose far more than others. Under these circumstances it is going to be difficult to secure agreement on appropriate targets and on the allocation of emissions reduction targets between countries. Furthermore, if global warming is reduced it will generally be of benefit to all countries, and no country can be excluded from the benefit. Any one country could secure the benefit of a global agreement without sharing in the cost: it could refuse to cooperate and wait for the rest of the world to solve the problem, i.e., it would become a "free rider." Whether a carbon tax or a marketable permit solution is the preferred mechanism is therefore, at this stage, somewhat premature. Some countries will be net losers, and it is difficult to see how they could be persuaded to cooperate, without compensating subsidies from the gainers.

There have been many efforts to estimate the costs of meeting various targets of greenhouse gas reduction. The studies vary considerably in terms of targets, timing, and country emphasis.[5] Most of them are applicable to the industrial countries, but some attempt to estimate global costs. For example a pioneering study in the United States by Nordhaus (1991) suggests that to achieve a 20 percent reduction in CO_2 emissions over the next 20 years, the cost per ton of carbon would range from zero to about

US\$28. Higher costs, largely dependent upon more ambitious or longer-term targets, or which are less ambitious about adaption prospects, have been estimated in several other studies.

Sometimes these estimates have been presented in terms of their implications for a carbon tax which, in effect, would be required to equilibrate marginal abatement costs with the marginal (global) benefits of the given reduction in emissions. For example, for the United States, Manne and Richels (1990), modeling energy-economy interactions explicitly, estimate how large a carbon tax would have to be to stabilize U.S. emissions at their 1985 rate through 2010, and then reduce emissions by 20 percent after this date. Their estimates indicate that the tax would have to peak in 2020 at US\$700 per ton of carbon, or US\$500 per ton of coal—more than ten times the actual price of coal in 1988. An estimate by OECD in 1991 is that to cut the output of CO_2 by 20 percent between 1990 and 2010 and stabilize it thereafter would need a tax in 2020 averaging US\$215 per ton of carbon (equivalent to US\$36 per barrel of oil). London Economics (1991), faced with the wide variety of models, assumptions, and targets, ran a regression on the results of the major studies, and came up with an average marginal cost for CO_2 reduction from 1988 levels by they year 2005 (the "Toronto target") of around US\$120 per ton of CO_2 reduced.

As noted, most of the above studies relate to industrial countries. A far more optimistic scenario is implied by the work of Sasmojo and Tasrif (1991) with regard to Indonesia. Their estimates suggest that, by taking advantage of opportunities for technology changes, and reducing energy intensity by price deregulation and imposing differential taxes on fossil fuels, substantial reductions in CO_2 emissions can be achieved with—at least in the short run—little impact on the economy. This finding, in common with

---

[5]For further details on these studies, see the Sri Lanka case study in Volume II.

other analyses in the same issue of *Energy Policy* in which it is presented, as well as other work done in the Asia region,[6] provide substantiation of the potential scope for "no regrets" policies in the developing world. The estimated magnitudes of such a tax vary widely according to target.

In considering the case for a carbon tax, the availability of alternative (untaxed) fuels should be addressed. The carbon tax might be counterproductive to the extent it might induce consumers to substitute wood, charcoal and crop residues (highly inefficient sources of fuel) for commercial sources. However, one advantage of a carbon tax is that it would reduce the emissions of other pollutants such as SO_2, not only because it would reduce energy consumption in general, but would also encourage substitution of cleaner fuels like natural gas for dirtier fuels such as coal.

Trade bans

Banning international trade in endangered species or other threatened resources is an explicit environmental policy, based upon command and control. For example, timber export bans have been used in developing countries, such as Indonesia, but the primary goal has been to protect domestic wood processing. Such policies raise generic issues about the role of market forces in achieving efficient solutions, both from an economic as well as environmental standpoint.

Proponents of trade bans argue that control is justified since trade of a specific commodity or product causes externality either in consumption (in the importing country) or in production (in the exporting country).

It is, however, often argued that trade bans may be counterproductive. Banning international trade in ivory, for example, has been criticized on the grounds that the commercial value of the elephant offers its best prospect for survival (Pearce and Warford 1993).

The international subsidy solution

The compensation approach can be illustrated at the international level by three examples:

(a) Payment by a country damaged by pollution to the country causing it. The costs of achieving marginal reductions in pollution increase rapidly as higher standards are reached. Consequently, marginal abatement costs in Eastern European countries tend to be lower than in the Western European countries, where standards are much higher. Where transboundary pollution exists, therefore, there are opportunities for Western European countries to subsidize pollution abatement in Eastern countries, and thereby achieve reductions in domestic pollution levels at relatively low cost.

(b) Debt for Nature Swaps, where special interest groups compensate countries for taking conservation measures in the perceived global interest.

(c) Global Environment Facility (GEF) Montreal Protocol, where the international community compensates countries for the incremental costs incurred in addressing global objectives.

Generic to all the above are problems inherent in provision of subsidies. These are similar to those observed at the domestic level: i.e., how to ensure that the subsidy will be used for the intended purpose (monitoring and compliance); measuring incre-

---

[6]See, for example, Phantumvanit and Panayotou 1990.

mental costs; game playing; and cost-effectiveness.[7]

Market-Based Instruments in OECD Countries

To date the use of market-based instruments for pollution control has been fairly limited in the industrial world. An OECD survey in 1987 of the range of market-based instruments used for pollution control in industrial countries concluded that while user charges (e.g., charges for water supply, landfilling waste, etc.) were widespread, specific environmental taxes were comparatively rare.[8] In general, the levels of these charges were rarely adequate to have any incentive effect. Indeed, rather than influencing environmental behavior, recovery of the administrative costs of regulation appears to have been the primary objective. Command-and-control, or regulatory methods were dominant. Moreover, of the 150 instruments identified, about 40 were in the form of subsidies, which in general run counter to the arguments in favor of market-based instruments.

Recognition of the important role that economic incentives can play in environmental management has become more apparent in recent years. Appropriate pricing and taxation structures are gradually emerging, although actual levels still generally fall well below those necessary to effect major behavioral change. In January 1991, guidelines for the application of market-based instruments (in conjunction with regulation) in environmental policy were presented at the ministerial meetings of the Environment Committee of the OECD. The announcement was partly motivated by the experience of OECD countries, indicating the feasibility of such instruments. It was also partly due to recognition of increased regulatory costs as environmental controls are further strengthened in industrial countries.[9]

Recent developments in the OECD countries indicate a substantial increase in the use of economic instruments since the 1987 survey, it being estimated that the number has increased by perhaps as much as 50 percent.[10] The important thing to note is that the instruments that have been introduced most frequently are product charges (otherwise known as presumptive charges), and deposit-refund systems. In the countries for which data are available, the increase in the use of these approaches have been 35 and 100 percent, respectively. However, their practical impact is somewhat difficult to assess. Emissions charges do not appear to be used more frequently now than they were in 1987, and there are in fact a limited number of convincing examples of successful application of emissions charges. Exceptions are the systems in place in Germany and the Netherlands, but these require highly sophisticated monitoring and enforcement capability.

Revenues from such charges are generally earmarked for environmental expenditure, and their role in creating incentives for improved environmental behavior continues to be small. On the other hand, tax differentiation in the automobile transport sector, in particular, with regard to leaded gasoline, has typically had an overtly environmental objective, and been aimed, with some success, at shifting production and consumption from leaded to unleaded fuel. User charges for waste collection and disposal and for sewerage and sewage treatment are common in OECD countries. Tradeable permits have also been introduced in the United States.

---

[7]Refer to Munasinghe and King 1991 on chlorofluorocarbons (CFCs).

[8]Opschoor and Vos 1988.

[9]See OECD 1991.

[10]As summarized in OECD 1993.

Specifically, some recent developments in OECD countries include the United Kingdom's announcement that it will increasingly rely upon environmental taxes and fees rather than command and control. Examples of actual taxes and charges aimed specifically at altering consumer and producer behavior include differential pricing of gasoline, with a higher price applying to gasoline containing lead additives. This has been adopted by France, Germany, Norway, Sweden, and the United Kingdom, while some other countries rely upon regulation of the maximum allowable concentration of lead in gasoline.

Other energy pollution taxes, typically based upon inputs rather than emissions (i.e., product or presumptive charges), are becoming increasingly advocated in OECD countries. Sweden has been a leader, having, for example, introduced the world's first carbon tax in 1991. In the energy sector the tax is levied on oil, coal, natural gas and liquid petroleum gas; in the transport sector the tax is imposed on gasoline, diesel and on domestic air traffic. A value added tax also applies to all fuels and electricity. Sweden also has a sulfur tax. France has announced plans for nitrogen oxide and sulfur dioxide taxes, and Italy and the Netherlands are considering the introduction of carbon taxes. With regard to air pollution from fuels, France has introduced charges on the sulfur content of fuels, and Finland and Sweden have charges on vehicle fuels. Finland and Germany have lubricant oil charges, while charges for solid waste, especially relevant for products that require recycling or safe disposal, are to be found in an increasing number of countries.

Agriculture input taxes, aimed at reducing chemical pollution, have also been introduced; once more, Sweden has taken the lead. It levies a special charge on nitrogen and phosphate fertilizers and another on the acreage of land treated with pesticides. Revenues raised by Swedish taxes are used for research in forestry, agriculture and environmental issues, but there is evidence that they have had some effect in reducing fertilizer and pesticide consumption.

Deposit-refund schemes, which are variants of pollution taxes, are now widely employed. When the product is purchased its price contains a tax which is then refundable on proper disposal or recycling of the product. Traditionally used for purely commercial purposes for beverage containers, this approach continues to be used for bottles and aluminum cans, and has been extended to car hulks in Norway, Sweden, and Germany.

Tradeable permits are employed in the United States for air pollutants, and were introduced for a limited period for lead in gasoline and for one case of effluent to a watercourse. The permit system introduced under the U.S. Clean Air Act is the most ambitious to date. The amount of trading activity between different polluters has been less than anticipated. This has possibly been due uncertainties regarding other firms' willingness to trade, the costs of obtaining regulators' permission to trade, uncertainty about just what emissions credits ensue under legislation, and uncertainty due to the prospect of rising permit prices. However, emissions trading either within firms or between firms have apparently resulted in considerable cost savings compared with a command-and-control approach.

Although the "polluter pays principle" is widely advocated, in fact, in many cases, governments actually provide subsidies to induce industry to cooperate in pollution abatement policy. Various forms of subsidy are to be found, and used either as purely political measures to ensure cooperation, or to alleviate short-term transition problems, such as the avoidance of industry closure or unemployment. Subsidies might take the form of low interest loans, tax breaks such as accelerated depreciation, or outright grants. Japan, for example, has had a comprehensive, and highly successful program of assisting small businesses to meet increasingly stringent environmental standards.[11] Subsidy programs (as U.S. experience indicates) clearly have major disadvantages. These include large administrative costs of ensuring that subsidies are used for the intended purpose, distortion of investment decisions where some expenditures qualify for subsidy while others do not, and of course the fiscal costs of the program.

Use of Market-Based Instruments in Developing Countries

Although the evidence is somewhat fragmentary, the following review of available material—which does not pretend to be comprehensive, but is at least illustrative—suggests that there are few cases in which explicit economic instruments are effectively used in developing countries, although they may have existed in a legal sense for some time. This is unsurprising in view of the slow rate of adoption of market-based instruments for pollution control in the industrial world. There are, however, signs that this situation is changing. Some examples are as follows.[12]

Emissions charges

Effluent charges for water pollution and emission fees for air pollution have been used for a number of years in China. In cases where pollutants discharged fail to meet state or local standards, an additional fee, based upon the amount and concentration of pollutants is levied. Until recently about 75 percent of the levy was actually returned to the enterprise, the balance being

used to finance the regulatory agency. Problems with this system have been due to the fact that the levy has been too low to be effective, enforcement has been inadequate, and there is little incentive to do more than just meet the minimum standard.

In Izmir and Istanbul, Turkey, sewer charges are assessed for industrial discharges into the sewer system, motivating factories to treat industrial effluents. Enterprises face both treatment and disposal costs (sewer charges). Charges are low relative to sewage collection and treatment costs. However, if they were much higher, the problem of illegal disposal would arise—a generic issue in environmental management. (A similar problem has been encountered in Sao Paulo, Brazil.)

In Poland, emission fees have been in existence for a number of years, but have not been effective. This has primarily been because enterprises have lacked the incentive to respond efficiently to such charges, because the price mechanism in general did not work. Also the levels of fees sometimes were too low to matter.

Some efforts have recently been made to introduce emissions taxes in some of the rapidly industrializing economies of Asia.[13] The air pollution prevention fee in Taiwan (China), will include an emission charge on stationary sources of air pollution, while in the Republic of Korea emission charges for air and water can be levied on enterprises whose emissions fail to meet legislated standards. Charges are, however, not related to the level of excess emissions nor is there an upper limit on the amount of the levy. As in China, there is therefore no incentive to do other than just avoid violation of the existing standards.

A review of a number of countries in Latin America also shows little evidence of effective use of emission fees, although four states in Brazil are in the process of intro-

---

[11]Aoyama et al. 1994.

[12]This draws upon Bernstein 1993, which should be consulted for further details on environmental management instruments in both industrial and developing countries.

---

[13]See O'Connor 1993.

ducing effluent charges for industrial sewerage based upon pollution content.[14] It is too early to judge the results of these policies. Brazil also has a system of fining violators of emissions standards, but the fines are not related to the damage done by actual emissions, and vary more according to frequency of violations rather than to toxicity or intensity. Similarly, in Buenos Aires, Argentina, discharge of waste into the air or water requires an operating certificate, without which fines may be imposed, depending on the level of violation. In practice, fines are so low that there is no incentive to adopt control measures. On the other hand, it has been found that fines set according to the severity of pollution have contributed to the control of surface water pollution in Mexico.[15]

Monitoring of emissions is of course considerably reduced if emission charges are restricted to a relatively few major dischargers of waste, and particularly if those dischargers are fairly homogeneous. A notable exception to the generally unsatisfactory experience with such charges is provided by Malaysia, which is of general relevance, and not simply for developing countries. In that country, the imposition of effluent charges for the palm oil industry helped reduce total pollutant loadings into water by a factor of almost 300 over the decade beginning in the early 1980s.[16]

Product (or presumptive) charges

Developing countries typically lack the institutional capability for implementing an environmental management system that relies heavily upon monitoring, inspecting, and regulating the activities of large numbers of polluters or other sources of environ-

[14]Margulis 1993.

[15]Quoted in Bernstein 1993.

[16]World Bank 1993f.

mental degradation, and in levying charges or fines. Even in industrial countries, this is a major problem, and one which applies equally to command-and-control systems as well as those based upon market-based instruments. Administrative realities therefore suggest the need to look beyond explicit, narrowly focused environmental interventions, particularly where pollution is caused by large numbers of waste dischargers. Blunter instruments, which can be introduced at a higher level in the economic system and which have pervasive impacts, not only upon environment, but on other aspects of development are more likely to be required in developing countries. The most direct approach is to make use of product or presumptive charges, which are based upon a presumed technical relationship between (a) certain inputs such as coal or gasoline which are used in production processes or final consumption, and (b) the environmental damage that is caused by these uses.

It is fairly apparent that developing countries lag behind the OECD countries in making effective use of such charges. Indeed, there remain many cases of where products which can be assumed to have adverse environmental health impacts when used are actually subsidized rather than taxed. Agricultural pesticides and fertilizers are perhaps the clearest example. Recent improvements in this regard, assisted by the introduction of integrated pest management systems in countries such as Indonesia are, however, encouraging. Similarly, the traditional subsidization of low quality (high-sulfur content) coal in China is now being phased out. Price differentiation, to reflect variations in environmental damage of otherwise similar products, has also recently been introduced to encourage the substitution of unleaded for leaded gasoline in a number of countries, including Thailand and Taiwan (China). Incorporation of sewerage pricing into water pricing can be seen as a form of product charge, this being further discussed below, as is the use of gasoline taxes in general. While documentation of the extent to which product charges exist is entirely inadequate, it does appear that many opportunities exist for reforms along the lines that are now being observed in the OECD countries, and that these should merit high priority.

Tradeable permits—rare in the industrial countries—are even less apparent in the developing countries. An exception is to be found in the case of Chile, where air pollution rights have been allocated to fixed sources in Santiago. Still in the process of evolution, the system allocates the maximum level of daily emissions, to be reached by the end of 1997. Any emission above the limit and below the emissions standard must be compensated by reduction of emissions from some other source. A number of administrative and other issues are still to be resolved, but this system appears to be developing quite well. Singapore has also introduced auctionable permit systems for rights to import and use ozone-depleting substances.

Deposit-refund systems

These are now being introduced in a number of non-OECD countries, particularly in the Asia region. For example, Korea and Taiwan (China), have recently introduced deposit-refund systems. These cover items such as food and beverage containers, pesticide containers, lubricant oil, plastics, and certain domestic appliances. However, deposit rates tend to be too low to achieve significant results. Nevertheless the administrative mechanisms are in place and this potentially could be a significant policy instrument.

User charges for solid and hazardous wastes

Solid waste operations in developing countries are commonly financed by local taxes, user charges, or some combination thereof. Charging for collection on the basis of volume of municipal waste disposed of might yield benefits, but problems of illegal dumping arise, as experience in a number of countries, such as Guatemala and Mexico, has shown. A more common approach is to incorporate a fixed charge into the local property tax. Monitoring and enforcement of such a system is in principle more straightforward for larger waste dischargers. Tipping fees for solid waste transfer and disposal are sometimes used, though problems of illegal tipping also constrain such a policy. For obvious reasons, discharges of hazardous and toxic wastes are usually subject to regulations, or outright bans, rather than to pricing instruments.

Subsidies

Although not well documented, it is believed that specific subsidies for environmental purposes are widespread. Typically these form part of a carrot and stick approach, in which they complement other economic or regulatory instruments. The Asia region again provides good examples.[17] Thus in Taiwan (China), Thailand, and Indonesia, various forms of subsidy are available for investment in pollution control equipment. Depending on the country, these may take the form of duty free imports, reduction in corporate income taxes, accelerated depreciation, low interest loans, and so on. While often a necessary price to pay to achieve the cooperation of industry in environmental management, subsidy programs are in general undesirable, not simply because they involve a fiscal burden for government, but also because they distort investment decisions. Even more prevalent than specific environmental subsidies are those sectoral subsidies which in effect

---

[17] O'Connor 1993.

subsidize environmental degradation, as noted in the next section.

While we do not find many examples of success stories in developing countries, trends in the industrial world do point toward strategies applicable to the poorer countries. A common theme throughout the debate on economic instruments revolves around their administrative feasibility. With regard to explicit policies, the OECD countries are increasingly emphasizing the use of product charges and taxes, which are administratively manageable, and therefore contrast with other economic or regulatory methods which depend upon continuous monitoring of large numbers of waste dischargers. The use of deposit-refund systems also appears to be on the increase in both developing and industrial countries, and administration of such schemes does not seem to have posed major problems.

Administrative simplicity is of particular importance in a developing country context, in which institutional capacity tends to be much less than in the industrial countries. In light of this, the following recommendations regarding the use of economic instruments in developing countries may be made. First, given the undoubted merits of emissions taxes, to identify the relatively few, large scale waste dischargers, and apply emissions charges to that group (i.e., the Malaysian palm oil industry example). Second, devote a major effort to the design and implementation of presumptive product charges and taxes—as well as deposit refund schemes—in the developing countries.

Conclusion: Role of Market-Based Instruments in Developing Countries

Green taxes

For governments faced with urgent fiscal needs, arguments in favor of environmental taxes are persuasive. Countries should explicitly consider the case for market-based

instruments, particularly those that generate public revenues. It should be noted that the general view is to regard the imposition of pollution or GHG taxes as a major impediment to growth, the analogy of the oil price increases in the 1970s and 1980s often being employed. However, as distinct from the latter case in which costs were exogenously imposed on oil-importing countries, opportunities are available to use the revenue generated for beneficial purposes. Indeed, environmental taxes may help to address fiscal concerns in two ways: not only do they generate revenue, but by discouraging environmentally damaging behavior in an efficient manner, they also reduce the need for environmental expenditure. From a fiscal point of view alone, the potential use of pollution taxes as a substitute for distorting taxes on effort and enterprise therefore merits close scrutiny in both developing and industrialized countries.

Subsidies

It follows that developing countries in particular should avoid subsidizing polluters. Such subsidies may have been acceptable in the past for certain industrial countries which have been able to stand the fiscal consequences and which have the administrative capability to avoid the abuses and distortions inherent in the provision of subsidies. This may have applied in the past to Japan, but this case is almost unique.

Market failure and government failure

As noted, governments rarely rely upon taxes as a major weapon in their environmental armory. Indeed, far from employing market-based instruments in a positive way, they often actively encourage environmentally degrading activities by subsidizing them.

Figure 2–3 presents a contrasting situation to that depicted in Figure 2–2. As illustrated here, a government subsidy lowers a firm's production costs, so MB is artificially increased to MB(s). Thus, private profit is everywhere greater than it was previously. The polluter expands production to Q3, and the total amount of external cost is even higher. Since subsidies are typically not justified in standard economic terms, this suggests that there is scope for bringing about environmental improvements that are justified in economic terms as well. In fact, as the next chapter demonstrates, there are many opportunities in developing countries for policy reforms which meet both economic and environmental criteria.

Administrative constraints: need for blunter instruments

In view of the slow rate of adoption of market-based instruments for pollution control in the industrial world, it is not surprising that there are few examples of such policies in the developing countries. Although the efficiency—or cost-effectiveness—arguments in favor of market-based instruments suggest that they should be seriously considered by developing countries, reform will not be accomplished immediately.

Developing countries typically lack the institutional capability for implementing an environmental management system that relies heavily upon monitoring, inspecting, and regulating the activities of large numbers of polluters or other sources of environmental degradation, and in levying charges or fines. Even in industrial countries, this is a major problem, and one which applies equally to command-and-control systems as well as those based upon market-based instruments. Administrative realities therefore suggest the need to look beyond explicit, narrowly focused environmental interventions. Blunter instruments, which can be introduced at a higher level in the economic system and which have pervasive impacts, not only upon the environment, but on other aspects of development are more likely to be required in developing countries. These are discussed in the next chapter.

In practice, environmental policy should typically consist of a combination of economic and regulatory instruments, aimed at the achievement of economic and environmental efficiency, and designed in light of the various political, institutional, and administrative constraints that each type of intervention involves. Whether regulatory or economic instruments are employed it is of course essential that they are soundly based from an engineering, chemical, biological, and epidemiological standpoint. Such expertise is required in the valuation of environmental damage, which should ideally be the basis for determining the level and structure of environmental standards or taxes.

The design of product charges and of responses in anticipation of the effects of macroeconomic policies also requires such skills. Inter alia, these require an understanding of the kinds of resources and materials used in industrial and agricultural processes or final consumption; the relationships between their utilization and the eventual discharge of waste material, and the technical processes by which they are transformed; the consequent impact upon the natural environment; and upon human health. Economic instruments, as well as regulatory ones, must be based upon a good understanding of such key technical relationships if they are to be effective. Quite apart from providing specific technical expertise, the above suggests that environmental advisers in both government and international agencies have an important role to play in bringing various disciplines together in the design of economic or other policy instruments.

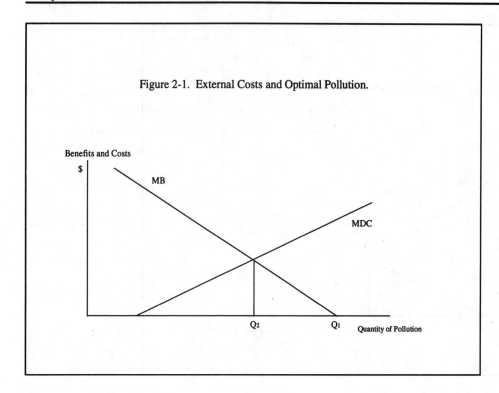

Figure 2-1. External Costs and Optimal Pollution.

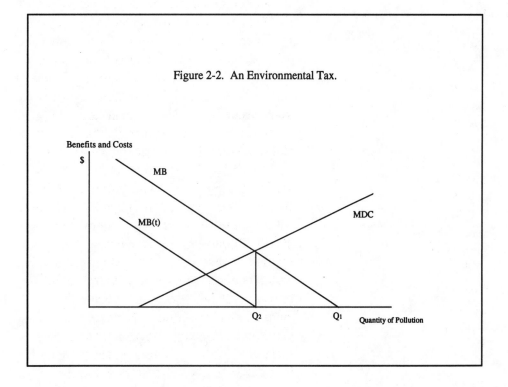

Figure 2-2. An Environmental Tax.

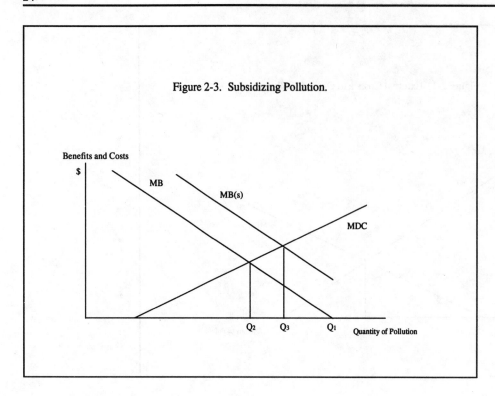

Figure 2-3. Subsidizing Pollution.

3

Sectoral Policies

"Win-Win" Policies

THIS CHAPTER IS CONCERNED WITH THE IMPLICATIONS of economic policies that are adopted for sectoral purposes but have wide-ranging impacts, including significant effects on resource use and the environment. These include policies, such as energy pricing, which have pervasive impacts on all other sectors, as well as policies with specific sectoral purposes, such as a combination of crop price supports and subsidies for fertilizer and credit designed to encourage agricultural intensification. The examples that follow demonstrate that the environmental consequences of sectoral policies and programs on the environment have been considerable, but often unanticipated.

These environmental consequences occur through production and consumption shifts due to changes in relative commodity prices or factor incomes associated with a wide range of sectoral policy reforms. Since many of these environmental effects are not reflected in market prices, very little systematic attention has been paid to these in the past.

This chapter is primarily about government or policy failure. In a definitional sense, the distinction between the subject of this chapter and that of Chapter 2 is somewhat artificial, since inadequate measures to address market failure can also be defined as government or policy failure. However, while the role of government may be viewed to be a passive one in not dealing with market failures, in the sectoral policy examples discussed below government policy takes a more active role in creating the distortions underlying the environmental problem. The distinction between explicit environmental interventions and sectoral policies is also not clear-cut. For example, policies on royalties in the mining sector and timber felling fees are both sectoral and environmental policies. However, in practice these policies have not been generally espoused for explicit environmental goals such as achieving an optimal level of resource exploitation. Most royalties, licenses, and charges are either nominal or established primarily for revenue generation, and they have limited if any contribution towards achieving sustainable resource management.

Central to the discussion is the concept of the "win-win" policy, i.e., a measure which meets both economic and environmental objectives. Due to widespread government inefficiencies, both in developing and industrial countries, many opportunities exist for policy reform that fall into the "win-win" category. Examples of such policies, as noted below, are to be found in the energy, industry, water resource, transportation, agriculture and forestry sectors. The mani-

festations are many and refer primarily to those policies which encourage wasteful resource use (i.e., consumption for purposes in which social costs exceed social benefits), resulting in excessive rates of depletion and pollution. Clearly, some ambiguity surrounds the definition of "economic" objectives, which do not always focus on efficiency goals and might legitimately encompass efficiency, fiscal, distributional and growth criteria. However, the many opportunities that exist for policies in which tradeoffs between environmental and other objectives are minimal, suggest that the appropriate strategy for developing countries as well as international development agencies should be to give high priority to policy reforms which pass "win-win" tests.

As a general example of the opportunities for such reforms, consider pricing policies. Just as pricing may be consciously aimed at the achievement of multiple objectives, inadequate attention to its often pervasive consequences may result in multiple, often unanticipated, consequences. From a societal point of view, the price of consuming a natural resource (including using it as a medium for disposal of waste) should equal its marginal opportunity cost (MOC). This price equals the sum of marginal private cost (MPC), marginal user (or depletion) cost (MUC), and marginal external cost (MEC)[1] or, if the resource is internationally traded, its border price, if this is greater. In practice, it is rare to find prices being set in this way; in fact, the situation depicted in Figure 3–1 is more common.

Ideally, in terms of Figure 3–1, price should equal P_1, i.e., equal to the border price, if the resource concerned is a trade-

---

[1]Note that MPC includes MUC when markets work perfectly. Also, MEC will be included in MPC where externalities are internalized by government intervention, for example, in the form of pollution taxes or regulations. Environmental costs are an important—often the dominant—component of external costs.

able. If not a tradeable, the MOC price would be P_2; the MPC price would be at P_3; average (financial) cost (AFC) pricing would be P_4. Setting price below MPC not only implies a financial subsidy which is a drain on public revenues, but also encourages excessive consumption, resulting in both waste of resources and environmental degradation.[2] It also creates "rent," i.e., the difference between the economic benefit obtained and the apparent cost of consumption, and therefore has distributional implications.

Such conditions are frequently encountered in developing countries where prices frequently fail even to reflect purely financial costs (AFCs) of production; i.e., they are at P5. While the optimal level of consumption—at least for a tradeable—is Q1, the actual level is Q5. Economic and environmental gains may therefore be achieved by simply ensuring that prices reflect financial costs of production. Raising prices to MPC, and still further to MOC, increases both economic and environmental gains. The final shift, to border price, achieves further efficiency gains only. The potential for "win-win" policy reform in this case is clear. We now consider the scope for such reform on a sector-by-sector basis.

Energy Sector

Numerous environmental problems are associated with energy consumption, including emissions of greenhouse gases and SO_2, water pollution, and the resettlement and ecological impacts of large projects, such as dam construction. Energy conservation has enormous potential, but it is not a panacea. Even under an energy efficient scenario, economic development will require substantial increases in fossil fuel consumption for the foreseeable future. Nevertheless, substantial progress in reducing energy needs

per unit of output as well as controlling the level of pollution per unit of energy generated can be achieved by combining the potential contribution of technical interventions with price reform. In past efforts at energy conservation and pollution control, there has been almost exclusive dependence on technical or regulatory approaches. This section highlights the potential impact of price reform that can eliminate wasteful consumption or switch energy use from low to high value uses.

In many countries' energy sectors, the major opportunity for immediate improvement, at little or no cost, lies in reform of electricity pricing policies. On average, developing country electricity prices are about one half of those in developed countries. Ideally (and assuming that marginal costs are defined to include those of depletion and external damages), price should be equal to both short-run marginal cost (SRMC) and long-run marginal cost (LRMC). However, in practice this may not be possible due to capital indivisibility. A pragmatic approximation, and one which recognizes that the true economic costs of incremental consumption imply bringing forward the need for additional investment in capacity, even if excess capacity currently exists, is to set price equal to average incremental cost (AIC).[3]

Kosmo's (1989) study of electricity pricing in developing countries showed that prices were invariably well below LRMC, the level at which an efficient allocation of resources would be achieved. In a more recent survey of electricity tariffs in 60 developing countries, tariffs were shown to have decreased between 1979 and 1988, from US\$0.052–US\$0.038 per kWh in 1986

---

[2] The assumption of increasing marginal costs is obviously necessary here.

[3] Sometimes referred to as "discounted unit cost," average incremental cost is the present worth of incremental system costs divided by the "present worth" of future consumption. For elaboration, see Saunders, Warford, and Mann 1977; this is also summarized in Meier (ed.) 1983.

dollars. These prices were less than half those prevailing in OECD countries even though average power supply costs in the developing countries assessed were higher than in OECD countries. Average tariffs for nearly 80 percent of the utilities concerned did not cover long run marginal costs.[4] Such low prices require enormous subsidies that represent major drains on government budgets. For example, the *World Development Report 1992* (World Bank 1992k) notes that energy subsidies exceeded US$150 billion annually in developing countries. For electricity consumption alone, the subsidies amounted to about US$100 billion per year, suggesting that both capital and energy sources were being wasted on a very large scale.

Prices are typically even below the average cost to the utilities, which are themselves commonly heavily subsidized through favorable interest rates, or fuel prices, or outright grants. Raising electricity prices to at least LRMC (or as an approximation, AIC) is a priority. More ambitiously, it should equal MOC, and as noted earlier, this might be facilitated by ensuring that external damage costs are included in the rate base, perhaps by employing charges which will stimulate switching to cleaner energy sources. For example, carbon taxes could encourage power utilities to switch from coal to natural gas.

Price reform will thus typically fall well into the "win-win" category. For example, the benefits from increased electricity tariffs would be twofold. The first would be efficiency gains, where the reduction in consumption due to higher prices may result in savings in capital and operating costs. It has been estimated that many developing countries consume about 20 percent more electricity than they would if consumers had to pay the true marginal cost of supply. Aside from reduced demand, it is likely in devel-

oping countries, where supply shortages are endemic, that there will be substantial transfers of electricity consumption to higher value uses. Where excess demand continues to prevail, an immediate impact upon emissions of pollutants would not be achieved since pollution arises from the generation side. However, once excess demand is alleviated, the future growth rate in emissions would be slowed.

Also, perhaps as significant, the immediate effect would be a reduction in pollution per unit of GNP. If LRMC pricing were used, Kosmo (1989) estimates the annual value of energy savings at US$9 billion for China and US$4 billion for India. Even in highly industrial countries, electricity policies also leave something to be desired. The savings for the United States, for example, from an application of LRMC pricing would be about US$60 billion annually. Even if total energy consumption is unchanged, price reform to recognize the additional cost of peak loads would reduce the daily variation in power use and would therefore yield both efficiency and environmental benefits if power authorities relied heavily upon old, inefficient plants at peak periods.

Other economic objectives, such as reduction of budget deficits or provision of social safety nets, may also be achieved by such reforms. Where, as is typical, LRMC of power supply is rising, efficient pricing will raise revenues in excess of average (financial) costs. In many developing countries electricity supply is being subsidized from public revenues, and there would be financial constraints on supply expansion.[5] Power generation projects currently have little incentive to generate revenue due to the subsidy traditionally provided by governments. Tariff structures can also be designed to ensure equitable treatment and facilitate access to service. One example would be the use of "lifeline rates" for

---

[4]Saunders and Gandhi 1993.

[5]Anderson 1990.

Box 3–1: Increasing Water Scarcity

Surface and groundwater sources have been deteriorating in quality or have been depleted in many urban areas throughout the world. Due to increasing scarcity, unit costs of water are rising rapidly, and are typically 2 to 3 times the current project cost (Bhatia and Falkenmark 1992):

- In Amman, Jordan, the average incremental cost (AIC) of supplying water when groundwater sources were still available was estimated to be US$0.41 per cubic meter. With declining groundwater availability, surface water sources are now being tapped, increasing AIC to US$1.33 per cubic meter.

- In Shenyang, China, groundwater sources have declined in quality, and water will have to be conveyed more than 50 kilometers from a surface source. This shift will mean an increase in per cubic meter water supply cost from US$0.04 to US$0.11.

- In Lima, Peru, long-term plans now estimate the AIC of water to be US$0.53 per cubic meter, compared to US$0.25 in 1981. The reason is that the traditional sources of groundwater are no longer available since the aquifer has been severely depleted, and interbasin water transfers will have to be made.

- In Mexico City, Mexico, there have been problems of lowering of water tables, and land subsidence, as well as water quality deterioration in the Mexico Valley aquifer. This has meant that water from the Cutzmala River now has to be pumped to an elevation of 1 kilometer, using a 180 kilometer long pipeline. The AIC is thus US$0.82 per cubic meter, which is 55 percent more than the cost from the previous source.

Source: World Bank 1993i.

---

poorer consumers. Finally, prices which reflect social costs will also be a stimulus to the search for more efficient and cleaner means of supplying and consuming energy.

Water Supply

As in the case of electric power, municipal water supply, both to domestic and industrial users is typically heavily subsidized, with prices well below even financial supply costs. This leads to excessive consumption and depletion of water resources, and generation of waste water. Unit costs of water, particularly for large urban areas, are rising rapidly almost everywhere, as convenient sources are exhausted, and water has to be brought in from ever greater distances. These distances range from 50 to more than 100 kilometers in metropolitan areas in many countries, requiring large investment costs for pipelines and pumping equipment. Some examples are described in Box 3–1.

A recent review of World Bank municipal water supply projects concluded that the price charged to end users was only about 35 percent of the average (financial) cost of supplying it. Internal cash generation provides only a small proportion of project costs—8 percent in Asia, 9 percent in Sub-Saharan Africa, 21 percent in Latin America and the Caribbean, and 35 percent in the Middle East and North Africa. There is little economic justification for overall subsidization of urban—or indeed rural—water systems. Generally the bulk of the water consumed in developing country cities is by a small number of relatively wealthy consumers—large residential, commercial and business users—who are well able to pay for it.[6] Indeed, the system is such that subsidized services have meant rationing, and many of the urban poor actually end up paying much more because they are forced to get their water from alternative sources. For example, in Jakarta, Indonesia, households without municipal water system connections, buy water from street vendors for US$1.5–US$5.20 per cubic meter, depend-

---

[6]See Warford and Julius 1977.

ing on the distance to the public tap. Similar findings have been reported in other urban areas, such as Karachi, Nouakchott (Mauritania), Dhaka, Tegucigalpa (Honduras), and Port-au-Prince, where low-income households who have no access to the municipal system end up paying as much as 25 to 50 times more per unit of water.[7]

Studies also show that charging the full economic cost for water where marginal costs are rising (i.e., where marginal cost is greater than financial cost), is practicable since consumers' willingness to pay for water connection is high. For example, a study recently completed by the World Bank on rural water supply in Brazil, Haiti, India, Nigeria, Pakistan, Tanzania, and Zimbabwe indicates that the cost of private household connections can be recovered by including an amortization charge in the monthly water bill. This considerable willingness to pay appears to be much more common than previously believed in many rural communities.[8]

The political acceptability of increasing charges for basic necessities will always be a concern. However, higher prices will also foster conservation among users so that there should be opportunities for government to ensure basic supply for those who are really disadvantaged. The large revenue yields that can be expected from higher water pricing could also be used to provide basic supply for low income groups, who could be charged a "lifeline rate" for basic needs.

One of the obstacles to employing a pricing system based upon volume consumed is that of measuring an individual's consumption. The "metering problem" (see Box 3–2) clearly arises with water supply, where the costs of measurement are high relative to the cost of consuming the product itself. As shown not only in the water supply sector itself,[9] but also, with regard to peak load pricing, for electric power,[10] the decision whether or not to meter is in fact amenable to sensible cost-benefit analysis. This is an important issue because of its generic relevance to the environment, in which the cost of exclusion is inherent in the resolution of externality or public goods problems.

Transportation

Typically, the transportation sector in developing countries is characterized by inefficiency, and is increasingly dominated by the private automobile. Traffic congestion and pollution are a growing problem. Many policies have contributed to this problem. For example, in Indonesia, subsidies for diesel fuel lead to air pollution and road congestion and damage. Similarly, the prevalence of low vehicle registration fees have encouraged congestion and pollution in many countries.[11]

Although most sectoral reform efforts in this area have been motivated by goals of reducing road damage and congestion and generating infrastructure maintenance revenues, there are indirect beneficial effects on air quality. Policies that encourage mass transit systems, such as railroads, also reduce energy use and emissions per commuter mile and therefore merit close scrutiny. In addition, since pollution-related effects are associated with emissions in densely populated areas, policies that discourage use of congested areas will also be beneficial. Thus, these reforms that are implemented for transport sector goals might also be expected to result in pollution reduction. In addition, they will also have nontransport

---

[7]World Bank 1993j.

[8]World Bank 1992k, pp. 6–7.

[9]See, for example, Middleton, Saunders, and Warford 1978.

[10]Munasinghe 1990.

[11]World Bank 1992d.

Box 3–2: *Measuring Resource Use—the Metering Problem*

The metering problem is generic for many types of resource or environmental management problems. Many services derived from natural resources and the environment have public goods characteristics. For example, air pollution control programs benefit people whether or not they pay for it. Other resource and environmental services—environmental amenities, tourism values, clean water—exhibit these characteristics to some degree. Irrigation water, for example, may be viewed as a quasi-public good in many developing countries. Canals, once constructed, cannot be limited only to farmers who pay irrigation fees. Secondary and tertiary ditches often traverse other farm land parcels before reaching the field of paying clients. Thus, farmers can directly tap into unlined or unprotected canals, and it may be very costly to exclude them. This introduces the problem of "free-riding" since potential users may attempt to reduce or altogether avoid paying for a share of environmental protection or resource investment costs.

Metering introduces the possibility of requiring potential users to pay for their use of resources or environmental services. Where marginal benefits for various categories of users differ, metering systems may provide the additional advantage of differential pricing. However, the cost of installing and monitoring such systems may exceed the social benefits of installing them. For example, the previous example of canal irrigation services suggests that volumetric metering systems will be prohibitively expensive. However, rotation-oriented metering of water use may provide some advantage over open access.

For municipal water supply, the potential savings may or may not outweigh the cost of providing meters for water use, depending upon (a) the incremental cost of water, (b) the impact of metering on water consumption, and (c) the cost of metering (Middleton, Saunders and Warford 1978). It should be noted that the sums involved are not trivial. In Mexico City, it has been estimated that the absence of metering and the prevalence of illegal water connections has led to a federal subsidy that exceeds US$1 billion annually. This is about 0.1 percent of gross domestic product (GDP) and equals the amount of annual sector investment needed to supply Mexico's water and sanitation needs to the end of the century.

Note the contrast in metering costs between water supply and electricity. In the latter case, metering costs are relatively low when compared to incremental capacity and energy costs. Thus, more sophisticated pricing—e.g., varying by time of day—may be economically justified for electricity supply.

---

sector economic contributions in terms of less traffic accidents, noise, and savings in commuting time and vehicle costs. Thus, fiscal, distributional, efficiency and environmental objectives might be achieved by policy reform in this sector.

Various means of bringing about improvement should be considered. Gasoline pricing reform seems to present the best opportunity since prices in developing countries average about US$1.25 per gallon, compared with US$3–US$4 per gallon in Europe and Japan. Other possibilities that should be considered include (a) imposition of a carbon tax, (b) congestion charges or restrictions on use of city centers, (c) and reform of policies which discriminate against fleet modernization.

Among the sectoral policies that have indirect environmental benefits listed above, those aimed at reducing traffic congestion are becoming increasingly popular. There

are many examples where congestion has been significantly reduced at low cost with the use of traffic management schemes. Such approaches include promoting mass transit, controlling on-street parking to increase traffic flow, and reducing the use of private cars (Armstrong-Wright 1992). A noteworthy example is the case of Singapore, which in 1975 introduced an area licensing scheme that required motorists to pay for a special license to enter the city's central business district (CBD) in the morning rush hour. The CBD includes about 620 hectares of Singapore where traffic congestion is greatest. In addition to the licensing scheme, Singapore also introduced a transport policy package that included: (a) free entry into the CBD by car pools, (b) higher parking fees in the CBD, and (c) progressively increasing taxes on car importation, purchase, and registration (Bernstein 1993).

The package contributed to significant reductions in automotive air pollution. The volume of private cars entering the CBD declined by 71 percent, and taxis decreased by about 65 percent. Car traffic started to rise again after 1977, but have remained significantly below pre-1975 levels. In conjunction with Singapore's other efforts in industrial pollution control and in promoting the use of more efficient cars, the impact on air pollution was significant. Total acidity, smoke, nitric oxide, and nitrogen oxide in the CBD declined, and the increase in carbon monoxide was moderated.

Policies that affect fleet modernization also have important environmental implications. In China, until the early 1980s trucks and cars had to be produced locally. With limited production, vehicle demand could not be met. Thus, the local fleet remained outmoded and was characterized by fuel inefficiency and excessive pollution.[12] Similarly, subsidies to mass transit may also have environmental advantages but have to be carefully assessed. Typically justified as a social service, mass transit subsidies may also contribute to reducing traffic congestion and air pollution (Heggie 1989). In China, rail transportation is favored over road transport. For hauling distances of about 100 km, transport tariffs for cargo are about four times more expensive by road than by rail. However, subsidies usually create other problems, aside from their immediate fiscal consequences, and environmental benefits need to be weighed against potentially broad distortions. For example, in China, the failure of freight rates to reflect costs spreads inefficiencies throughout the economy, affecting all sectors.

Industry

Efforts to promote industrial growth, whether through direct subsidies or through industrial protection, may have important implications for resource use and the environment. Some of the links are quite direct. For example, low energy prices are often justified in development planning on the basis of providing cost advantages to industry. This leads industrial expansion into energy-intensive product lines or technology choice. Similarly, the impacts of industrial tax/subsidy programs and trade policy might be reviewed to check the extent to which they discourage innovation; protect old-fashioned, inefficient industry; or discourage development of backstop technologies.

Many countries promote the development of resource-processing oriented industries by directly subsidizing investments or by controlling the prices of their raw materials. Investment subsidies may be implemented in the form of tax credits, subsidized loans, and tariff exemptions on the importation of capital equipment. The costs of raw materials are often controlled indirectly, by preventing producers from exporting their products or levying taxes on their export. The taxation of log exports (described below) is one of the more common examples of this effect. In this case the domestic price of the raw material for the forest industry sector, timber, is reduced significantly below world market prices. In contrast to "win-win" policies that promote gains in both efficiency and the environment, these industrial protection policies lead to inefficiency for the protected industry and to increased resource exploitation.

Direct industrial subsidies may, however, have both beneficial and negative environmental impacts. The negative aspects are illustrated by studies on Eastern European countries, demonstrating how centralized planning systems have led to excessive industrial pollution. In many of these countries, overinvestment in energy-intensive

---

[12]World Bank 1992c.

heavy industry, relatively few (or poorly enforced) environmental regulations, and an overriding concern to meet production targets, often at the cost of the environment and health and safety issues, have been instrumental in producing the highest levels of sulfur dioxide emissions in the world (Hughes 1992; chapter by Bates, Fiodor, and Gupta in Volume II). All these pollution studies illustrate the unanticipated effects of industrial regulation and protectionism on air pollution.

One important example of the potential beneficial effects of direct industrial subsidies is in eco-tourism, which in most developing countries primarily serves a foreign market. Where tourists may be attracted to a country to visit a unique nature park or site, government subsidies for managing or improving such sites could generate both economic and environmental benefits. In many cases, institutional reforms, designed to ensure that more of the revenues from tourism are actually used to protect and enhance the natural environment, are required. See, for example, Lindberg (1991).

Agricultural Commodities

Tax and subsidy policies are often associated with government efforts to promote agricultural production or to stabilize prices. Subsidies are introduced during periods when international crop prices are low, and crops are taxed when prices are high. The direct income benefits of price stabilization are probably limited, although there would be additional benefits if stabilization policies reduced risk-related constraints to agricultural investment.[13] Promoting investment will also be good for the environment if a more stable decisionmaking context leads to more conservation.

Using the example of smallholder producer prices in Malawi, Barbier (1991) examined the incentive effects of fluctuating relative prices on land degradation. The study indicated that crop pricing policies can have an important influence on land management in general if there is an effect on relative price fluctuations. Fluctuations in relative crop prices and returns reduced the incentives for smallholders to invest in improved cropping systems and land management by increasing the degree of price risk. The risk arising from fluctuating prices is not conducive to improving farming systems, incorporating new crops or investing in improvements in cropping patterns, cultivation practices, and conservation efforts.

In addition to the general effect of price fluctuations on land management, the extent of fluctuations may also differ among crops, and government intervention will have land quality implications depending on whether price stabilization ends up encouraging crops that promote more stable soil conditions, such as groundnuts and pulses, versus the more erosive crops, such as maize. If policies allow greater fluctuations among the former crops, they may further reinforce the general disincentive to improved farming systems and land management among poor farmers.

Aside from price policies leading to unanticipated substitution-type effects, one problem with many price stabilization efforts is that price support subsidies are often inadequate during periods of low prices. By contrast, when crop prices are high tax policies tend to be more effective. Indeed, due to revenue generation goals, such taxes often tend to be institutionalized, leading to a long-term bias against agricultural output and incomes. This creates the underlying basis for income effects that can have significant environmental implications.

---

[13]The problem with many price stabilization efforts is that price support subsidies are often inadequate while revenue generating taxes tend to be institutionalized, leading to a long-term bias against agricultural output and incomes.

In another example for Malawi, Cromwell and Winpenny (1991) showed that government efforts to provide crop price supports were ineffective and the actual prices received by many small farmers were substantially less than the statutory marketing board prices. Legislation also prevent smallholders from competing with estates in producing more profitable plantation crops. These policies depressed rural incomes, but farmers were also effectively prevented from seeking nonagricultural employment since the government also strictly controlled rural to urban migration. These policy constraints, coupled with a high population growth rate, led to the expansion of cultivation into marginal areas and a long-term decline in soil fertility.

The authors then assessed the impact of reforms implemented in the 1980s. The study examined both the estate and small farm sectors, and evaluated policy impacts in terms of changes in four environmental aspects: the extensive frontier of cultivation, intensity of production, product mix, and production technique. In an effort to respond to changes in producer prices and maintain real incomes, smallholders intensified production of food in marginal lands. However, estates were more responsive to improved trade conditions and export incentives. It was noted that the environmental effect of production changes depended on the crop being adopted and cultivation methods being practiced. The study concluded that, on balance, product mix had been the most sensitive to changes in prices and incentives. Land used for maize declined responded to the decline in returns to maize relative to export crops. When export incentives improved, the output of groundnuts and beans rose. Since the production of groundnuts and beans is probably more beneficial to soil fertility, relative to maize farming, the environmental effect may have been positive.

These observations on Malawi indicate that the particular characteristic of crops that are either promoted or discouraged have crucial environmental implications. This point has also been made in the context of indirect incentives for various crop activities in West Africa. Differential rates of implicit taxation among crops significantly affect land use, and many countries in Sub-Saharan Africa have historically discriminated against export crops relative to domestic food crops. This may appear to be environmentally beneficial since many environmentalists have presumed that export crop promotion aggravate soil erosion. However, it has been argued that this view is not generally valid since many export crops tend to be less erosion-prone than food crops.[14]

Most export crops are usually tree crops or perennials that provide land cover and more stable root structures. Examples are coffee, cocoa, rubber, palm oil, and bananas. Citing data for West Africa, Repetto (1989) concludes that where tree and bush crops are grown with grasses as ground cover, soil erosion rates form tree and bush crops may be up to three times less than the rates for crops such as cassava and maize. Thus, trade-oriented reforms could have beneficial implications not only for export growth but also for decreased environmental damages from soil erosion.

Agricultural Inputs

Irrigation

Irrigation schemes have been a main component of many agricultural development programs, and for a variety of reasons, including the compensation farmers require due to government intervention in product markets, they have also tended to be heavily subsidized. There are indications, however, that much of this subsidy has been unnecessary, and instead has discouraged efficient water use and conservation. Repetto (1986)

---

[14]Repetto 1989, pp. 71–72.

examined the consequences of water under-pricing in terms of the resultant inefficient performance of public irrigation systems in developing countries and in the United States. In this study, it was found that only 10 to 20 percent of the investment and operating cost of irrigation systems in many poor countries is actually charged. Both efficiency and distributional effects were negative since the subsidies led to excessive water use and the primary beneficiaries tended to be the better off farmers.

Changes in the water table and increasing land salinity are the most common environmental results of excessive water use. For example, irrigation subsidies were introduced in Peru in the 1970s to offset the decline in land improvements associated with the land reform program. Most public investments were directed at large irrigation projects in the Costa region (versus the Sierra and Selva). Low water fees and inadequate maintenance of these systems led to inefficient water use. The resulting soil salinization caused a loss of productive agricultural land. It is estimated that about 40 percent of agricultural land in the Costa region has been affected by salinity.

In many instances, such subsidies may not be really needed. This is suggested by studies of privately supplied irrigation water. In Bangladesh, farmers normally pay 25 percent of their entire dry season crop revenues to nearby tubewell owners who supply them with irrigation water. In Nepal, assessments of farmer-owned and managed irrigation systems have found that farmers are willing to contribute substantial amounts of cash and labor to pay for the costs of system operation and maintenance. For example, in six hill systems, the average labor contribution was about 50 man-days per hectare per year, and monetary contributions averaged about the equivalent wages for one man-month of labor.[15]

Beyond the current concerns with inefficient use of increasingly scarce water resources, there remains the long-term problem of declining productivity of irrigation systems due to environmental degradation. Up to the early 1970s, the tradeoffs between current demands to expand irrigated areas versus the long-term effects of irrigation were not considered a priority. Thus, many projects in the past 25 years were economically justified because expensive components such as drainage systems were not included (Barghouti and Le Moigne 1991). Since such systems may eventually suffer from declining yields due to waterlogging and salinization, irrigation programs may have contributed to the general pattern of transferring the costs of development from the present to the future.

Pesticides and fertilizers

Subsidies for pesticides and fertilizers are usually assumed to be detrimental to the environment because they favor the production of crops with high nutrient requirements, and they cause water pollution from runoff. Subsidies for pesticide use are substantial in many developing countries. Measured as a proportion of pesticide retail cost, the subsidies for eight countries studied have ranged from 19 percent in China to as much as 89 percent in Senegal.[16] Subsidies for chemical fertilizers have also been linked to possible environmental problems. Repetto has argued that such subsidies artificially reduce the incentives to practice soil conservation and have made farmers adopt short-sighted output-oriented strategies. In the 1960s such subsidies may have been important factors in promoting the use of "green revolution" technology, but the rate of fertilizer use has more than quadrupled in the last two decades. Subsidies in the 1980s normally constituted 50–60 percent of

---

[15]World Bank 1993i.

[16]Repetto 1985, Table 2, and pp. 19–27.

delivered cost and reached 80–90 percent in some countries.[17]

As in the case of crop pricing policies, the environmental implications of input subsidies need to be evaluated on a case-to-case basis. In instances when fertilizer use is very limited and soils are not productive, there may be a case for subsidy. An OECD study for Nigeria argues that fertilizer use in that country is substantially below what would be optimal (OECD[18]). Similarly, in Malawi, soil fertility was declining due to population pressure, maize mono-cropping and restricted availability of organic manure within the farming system. At the same time, effective fertilizer costs were increasing rapidly, due to oil price rises and the closure of transportation routes. This led to fertilizer, hectarage, and maize yields remaining static, and maize sales to government agencies fell dramatically. The reintroduction of a fertilizer subsidy in 1987 appears to have been environmentally benign under these circumstances, as it reduced the long-term decline in soil fertility that would otherwise have resulted (Cromwell and Winpenny 1991). Indeed, some authors take a much more positive view of the long-term contribution of agricultural chemicals. Stryker (1989), in a paper on the arid and semiarid tropics, proposes the retention of fertilizer subsidies in countries where soil depletion is a significant concern.[19]

Livestock

The decline of traditional tenure systems has resulted in open access conditions and subsequent land degradation in many grazing areas. Actual measurements of soil erosion and land degradation are seldom available. However, changing land cover conditions and dramatic declines in productivity are indicative of the extent of the problem. For example, in western Africa serious problems of pasture degradation due to overgrazing are reported in Togo, Cameroon, Guinea, and Cote d'Ivoire.

One of the best known examples of government failure in this sector was the policy of the Brazilian government of providing forest land, free of charge, for cattle ranching (Mahar 1988). Additionally, generous tax incentives were given for individuals to engage in cattle ranching. This development-oriented policy proved to be unsuccessful on both economic and ecological grounds. The negative environmental impacts were dramatic since prospective ranchers were required to completely clear forest lands in order to stake out their claim. Unfortunately, the program was also uneconomic since most ranching operations turned out to be unsustainable owing to the fragile conditions of Amazonian soils. Reform in this area is clearly a "win-win" policy, the present one failing fiscal, efficiency and environmental tests.

In an analysis of government livestock policy in Botswana, Perrings et al. (1988) demonstrate that a mix of policies constitute the underlying causes of rangeland degradation. The incentive structure prevailing in the country at the time of the report encouraged inefficient stocking and farm management decisions, resulting in rangeland degradation. These included the prices paid to producers, the system of subsidies, the tax structure, and the nature of property rights—all of which made the overstocking of grazing land privately rational even though the social costs in terms of degraded lands and unsustainable livelihoods were very high. Rangeland degradation results from the combined effects of soil erosion, depletion of soil nutrients, increasing soil aridity, and other factors, particularly drought.

---

[17]See, for example, Repetto 1989.

[18]Fontaine and Sindzingre 1991.

[19]In Leonard (ed.) 1989.

Livestock and crop prices were at artificially elevated prices due to the influence of high prices in the EEC countries and in South Africa. Simultaneously, real input prices for livestock and food crops were reduced due to domestic agricultural assistance programs. The impact of these price incentives was compounded by the presence of macroeconomic incentives to direct foreign investment, such as maintaining an undervalued exchange rate. All of these factors contributed to the incentives to add to herd sizes. To address the problem, the authors conclude that a comprehensive set of remedial policies will be required, including: (a) the introduction of a range levy, (b) charges for water use, (c) modification of tax benefits available on livestock, (d) setting producer prices at high enough levels to encourage an increase in offtake, and (e) subsidizing voluntary herd reductions in severely degraded areas.

Fisheries

In fisheries, government programs have been primarily motivated by production goals. There were attempts in the 1970s to duplicate the green revolution approach in agriculture by providing credit for boats, motors, and improved fishing nets and gear (Lockwood and Ruddle 1976). However, in fishing areas where there was already significant fishing effort and harvest was near the fisheries' maximum sustainable yield, such "blue revolution" programs merely served to increase overfishing. This process is documented in San Miguel Bay, one of the traditional fishing areas of the Philippines, where increasing fishing effort in the late 1970s was associated with declining yields by the early 1980s (Cruz 1986). The growth of communities dependent on the fishery, the open-access nature of the resource, and the production-oriented policies adopted by government contributed to overexploitation of the fishery.

Aside from labor and capital, fishery production is crucially dependent on the existing fish stock (or biomass). Since it is a biological resource, it experiences net growth through fertility or recruitment and mortality. The employment of labor and capital in the fishery (usually termed "effort") not only produces the catch but may also lead to an increase or reduction of the biomass available for the next fishing period. The biomass will increase or decline, depending on whether catch is less than or greater than the net growth for that period. The concept of sustainable yield therefore goes beyond the conventional notion of long-run production since the long-term trend in the level of biomass is directly affected by short-run harvesting activity. In the short run, any catch is theoretically feasible up to the level of available biomass, but this catch is not sustainable if biomass left over for the next period is already too limited.

Fishery biologists have long known that there is usually a maximum sustainable yield that is possible from a fishery, and this is associated with a given level of biomass and fishing effort. In some fisheries, the biomass level is primarily dependent on environmental conditions and not on the previous year's level so that with increasing fishing effort, catch may just stabilize instead of decrease (Anderson 1980). In either case, average catch will tend to decline, and this has been the basis for the standard recommendation in capture fisheries for limiting effort. Thus, conventional fishery management activities focus on restricting allowable gear or in limiting fishing area or season. Minimum net mesh size rules to protect immature fish is a common example of the first approach. Enforcing both types of schemes, however, is extremely difficult due to the large jurisdictions concerned as well as the number of fishermen involved. Limited entry schemes have therefore been proposed in attempts to minimize the need for command-and-control approaches by addressing the open access problem that dominates the incentive structure in fishing.

The basic economic argument for controlling fishing effort is that the open access to the resource dissipates the rent that may be potentially generated by resource use, as ever increasing numbers of fishermen overexploit the fishery. Limiting the amount of fishing activity and allocating these quotas will therefore prevent overfishing. In addition, those who are assured of the rights will have an interest in actively promoting fishing regulations and enforcing the quota, since the fishery as an asset will become more valuable to them.[20] The difficulty, of course, lies in how to allocate rights to fish. Nontransferable quotas or licenses to fish have been the traditional approach, but there is increasing experimentation in making these licenses transferrable and then auctioning them off to allow the management authority to capture resource rents. Some form of limiting entry will clearly be preferred to the current open access situation since harvests can increase and be sustainable.

Forestry

Policy for efficient and sustainable forestry in many developing countries is in its infancy since the multiple economic and environmental services provided by forests have only recently become widely recognized. Multiple uses and competing demands characterize forestry resources in many developing countries. The main forest products users are loggers and fuelwood gatherers. Agriculturists seek to convert forests into upland farms or pastures. Finally, government attempts to coordinate these conflicting demands so that the protective and amenity values of forests are preserved, while allowing for continued agricultural growth.

Since most forest lands in the developing world are under some form of government ownership and management, government policies significantly affect the rate of forest exploitation as well as the conversion of forest lands to agriculture (Hyde, Newman, and Sedjo 1991). There is considerable need for institutional and sectoral policy reforms, including control of logging operations and capture of economic rents from forest concessionaires, and measures to curb the highly inefficient use of wood for fuel. Continuing policy and institutional failures are associated with forest resource undervaluation and inadequate systems of forest land tenure, and these result in tangible economic losses, including lost export earnings from forest products, foregone government revenues, soil degradation and reduced agricultural productivity, and flooding.

Repetto and Gillis (1988) have analyzed the deforestation implications of the undervaluation of timber resources. While governments claim substantial social value of forests, the stumpage fee or charges for harvested timber is often nominal. Logging concessionaires can therefore capture enormous rents since they are able to export timber at a very high price. Because of this incentive structure, loggers are often motivated by rent-seeking to acquire as much timber harvesting concessions as possible, resulting in ever increasing pressure on timber resources (Cruz and Delos Angeles 1988).

Aside from logging, the other crucial source of deforestation is the conversion of forests to agricultural activities. In general, this process is the result of increasing demand for farm land from a growing population. The problem is exacerbated by the failure of centralized management systems, both in keeping new settlers from forest lands and in providing those who have already colonized such lands with the insti-

---

[20]Having no restrictions on entry is formally equivalent to an extreme undervaluation of the economic contribution of the fishery asset.

tutional structure that can encourage conservation-oriented farming practices.

This perspective has motivated continuing evolution in the World Bank's forestry policy. In its 1978 Forestry Policy Paper the emphasis shifted from industrial forestry and timber utilization toward social and rural development issues and environmental forestry. This followed from the recognition of the problem of timber undervaluation, a common policy distortion in many developing countries, as the source of deforestation and inappropriate land conversion. The problem of encroachment in forests, associated with poverty and degradation, was also identified in the 1978 policy paper although this was not emphasized. This major change in sectoral priorities led to efforts at "new style" forestry projects that incorporated watershed management and environmental activities.

The 1991 World Bank forest sector policy paper (World Bank 1991b) shifted the focus further and identified the relationship between deforestation and poverty and population pressure as the primary resource management concern. The need for zoning and regulations, correct economic incentives, and the role of public investment and research were the other priorities identified in the policy paper. Although the 1991 policy paper emphasized the problem of agricultural extensification and migration to forest land, analytical work that can improve current understanding of the mechanisms by which poverty and population affect deforestation have been limited. Two notable initiatives in this area are in Africa. As part of the Managing Agricultural Development in Africa (MADIA) program, Lele and Stone (1989) focus on a post-Boserup concept of policy-led agricultural intensification. Demand-led agricultural intensification (in the induced innovation tradition of Hayami and Ruttan 1971) has apparently not been as effective in Africa as in Asia and Latin America. The authors hypothesize that

with population pressure there will be a shift to the most productive (lowland agricultural) areas. However, this may be misdirected to forest or frontier lands by disease, economic policies, and inequitable land distribution.

A second study looks more generally at the "nexus" of trends in population growth, agricultural stagnation, and environmental degradation in Africa (Cleaver and Schreiber 1991). They find that shifting cultivation and grazing in the context of limited capital and technical change cannot cope with rapid population growth. At the same time, the traditional technological fix from the development of high yielding crop varieties are not available. Thus, they identify the need for a mix of responses in terms of reforms to remove subsidies for inappropriate land uses, improve land use planning, recognize property rights, provide better education, and construct appropriate rural infrastructure to promote production incentives.

With respect to the pattern of poverty and degradation, more work remains to be done on the problem of encroachment of forest lands by displaced farmers. Providing tenurial security is a key aspect of the problem. For farmers already in forest areas and marginal lands, providing security of tenure through a land reform program is the first step in encouraging conservation-oriented farming. In most instances, land reform is politically difficult to implement (Anderson and Thampapillai 1991). However, the problem of encroachment will often occur in public lands instead of private agricultural lands. Thus, alternative land reform in the public domain might be more workable.

One of the most comprehensive work done to date on the requirements for sustainable forestry management was the assessment of Philippine forestry presented in World Bank (1989a). This study, undertaken in cooperation with the government's Department of Environment and Natural Resources, identified the sectoral pricing and taxation reforms needed for improved commercial forestry management as well the institutional reforms needed to address the problem of population pressure on public forest lands. Philippine forest lands have declined from about half of the country's land area in the 1950s to less than 25 percent. Timber stumpage undervaluation, which provided substantial potential rents for loggers, for many years created excessive demand for control of forest concessions. At the same time, rapid growth of migrant communities contributed to the conversion of forest lands to agriculture. The study concluded that parallel reforms in timber pricing and in introducing community-based or decentralized approaches to forest land management should form the key components of any strategy for sustainable management.

Regional Aspects of Sectoral Policies

Regional development programs, which for our classification purposes fall somewhere in between sectoral and macroeconomic influences on the environment, often have massive and largely unanticipated consequences for the environment. This may be illustrated by reference to a number of programs, some of which have been highly publicized, such as the outer islands transmigration program of Indonesia, Carajas in Brazil, and Narmada in India. Because regional development projects substantially modify settlement and resource use patterns within their scope of influence, their environmental effects are often considerable. However, in many instances, these effects like social and institutional constraints are not anticipated in the design of projects and eventually contribute to problems in the long term. The examples above illustrate the variety of environmental effects that are often associated with large-scale regional

development projects. They indicate that more care must be taken to recognize the variety of local circumstances and resources that could be affected by the program. Planned resettlement efforts, as in Indonesia, unfortunately seldom evolve as planned. The long-term sustainability of new resources that are opened up for exploitation, as in Zambia, is often sacrificed for immediate returns. Formal industrial investment projects, as in Carajas, will often attract spontaneous ancillary activities, some of which may lead to environmental problems. Unfortunately, few government implementation agencies are capable of responding in a relevant and timely manner to such problems.

Global Environment Implications of Sectoral Policies

Sectoral policies in the energy sector, such as power pricing and choice of generation technology and inputs, have crucial environmental implications that go far beyond national boundaries. In turn global environmental concerns will normally transcend the interests of individual countries. This can be illustrated by GHG emissions. Scientific and economic uncertainties, difficulty of valuation, and the fact that global climate change is determined by policies and activities outside their borders, make it reasonable for developing countries to take the position that they will not take measures to address the GHG issue unless it is in their own economic and social interest to do so. Where, as in the case of GHGs, long-term benefits of control might be in conflict with urgent poverty alleviation objectives, this is a particularly powerful consideration.

The diagram below illustrates the situation facing a single country. (See Figure 3–2.) The MAC curve refers to the net marginal abatement cost to the country of each new method of reducing (or sequestration of) GHGs. MAC is the sum of the costs of introducing policy reform or emissions-reducing investments, *minus* any benefits which result from such expenditures, and therefore represents the net costs of alternative measures. (Alternatively, therefore, up to point A, MAC could be mirrored by the dotted curve MBC, or net marginal benefit to the country concerned). Clearly, countries intending to reduce GHG emissions should select the most efficient (i.e., cost-effective) options first. MAC therefore increases, the greater the percentage reduction in carbon dioxide emissions. The portion of MAC lying in the negative range (O-A) represents opportunities for "win-win" actions by the country.

Point A represents the level at which it is no longer in the interest of the country to reduce GHGs any further, i.e., at that point the costs of so doing exceed the benefits accruing to the country. However, there is a benefit to the world at large from such reduction. The global optimum emissions level therefore requires a greater emissions reduction than for the country alone. A global marginal benefit curve, MBG, would intersect MAC to the right of level A, i.e., at B. This would represent the global optimum, i.e., where global marginal benefits equal global marginal costs.

Assuming that all "win-win" opportunities are taken by the countries concerned, using conventional financing sources, GEF financing should in principle be restricted to the range A–B. Beyond that, further reduction in CO_2 emissions would not be justified even when global considerations are included. In view of the massive costs of arriving at the global optimum (as noted in the previous chapter), it is clear that any hope of moving significantly in this direction will depend heavily upon the implementation of sectoral policy reform—justified in their own right—at the country level.

Sectoral Policies and General Market Imperfections

This chapter has provided a flavor of the kinds of sectoral policies which might have an adverse environmental impact, but which also merit reform in their own right. Numerous obstacles obviously have to be overcome if policy reform is to be achieved; reduction in long standing subsidy programs or increases in the prices of goods and services supplied by government, or over which government has control, is notoriously difficult. In addition, economic theory itself often suggests that immediate pricing reform in a particular sector should be treated with caution. First, in the short run, demand may be inelastic, requiring considerable increases in prices to bring about change. Price reforms may also be politically unacceptable, and therefore ultimately counterproductive.

Second, reform of pricing or introduction of what may appear to be, at first sight, a move toward economic efficiency in any particular sector of the economy may in fact be a move away from it if optimal conditions do not prevail elsewhere; i.e., a "second best" policy may be called for. For example, the introduction of economic incentives in a sector—perhaps dominated by parastatals—may in fact be an inferior substitute for command and control, if economic incentives in general do not prevail in that sector. Or, as noted earlier, a tax on commercial energy may simply result in switching consumption to untaxed fuels, and elimination of agricultural input subsidies may have undesirable environmental and economic side effects.

A major constraint is therefore imposed by general market imperfections. Bringing about reforms at the sector level may be counterproductive in the absence of major economic policy reforms in the rest of the economy. As illustrated in subsequent chapters, the second best issue is a pervasive problem in the developing world, especially in China and in Central and Eastern Europe. General market imperfections might reduce the effectiveness of sector-specific policies, in particular when they rely upon market-based instruments. Their introduction will therefore often best be phased to conform with general trends in market liberalization. However, the relationships between such wide-ranging policies and the environment are much less well understood than sectoral policies.

For example, numerous exogenous influences—political, economic, and environmental—determine the appropriateness of general agricultural policy. Over time, governments have introduced an array of economic and other policies to react to these influences, and these measures have often created constituencies supporting the status quo, and which create obstacles to reform. They also give rise to the "second best" problem, which runs through the reform process, and is illustrated extremely well in the case of agriculture. Thus, proposals to reform, say, irrigation pricing, must be addressed in light of the whole range of distortions that characterize agricultural markets.

Conclusions

There is ample opportunity for "win-win" policies, but formidable obstacles to their implementation abound, largely because of the incidence of the costs and benefits of reform measures. It is to be hoped that policy reforms which are justified on their own merits might gather additional support when environmental concerns are weighed in the balance, and this coordination of conventional and environmental goals should be a central objective not only of the countries themselves but also of donor agencies.

Getting to market prices is in many cases a necessary first step in correcting distortions, to be followed by further correction in the direction of social cost pricing. The latter requires analysis of divergence between market and social costs and benefits, which can involve severe measurement problems. These arise not only because it is inherently difficult to place monetary values on environmental impacts,[21] but also because prediction of the physical impacts themselves is fraught with uncertainty. For example, subsidization of pesticides may have both positive and negative environmental effects, and socially and environmentally efficient energy pricing may be difficult to determine in practice. However, while precision may be difficult to achieve in such assessment, the general direction of needed reform will often be intuitively clear. The magnitude of underpricing is often so large that refinement of social cost calculations is of purely academic concern.

Indeed, while raising prices certainly raises various administrative problems (e.g., evasion of payment), the structure for recovering costs of water and electricity consumers already exists. Moreover, reduction in subsidies actually involves a dismantling of the administrative structure involved. Achievement of social cost pricing for key resources is therefore a feasible policy in both industrial and developing countries. Governments also often have the means to effect approximate adjustments for external cost—e.g., by raising gasoline taxes to account for vehicle air pollution, congestion and noise. Tariff levels and structures for water supply and energy are, in an administrative sense, quite possible to adjust. In general, therefore, while considerable research still needs to be done in this area, it is reasonable to expect policymakers to incorporate environmental considerations more systematically into decisionmaking at current levels of knowledge. Lack of precise information should not be an excuse for inaction.

---

[21]See Munasinghe 1993a.

It is also administratively quite straight-forward to introduce complementary blunt instruments, to cover the costs of sewerage, or of the damage done by utilization of high sulfur coal or gasoline. Finally, while macroeconomic policy reforms may be the most powerful of instruments, in view of their countrywide and cross-sectoral impacts, they are also the bluntest of instruments, and impact on all aspects of life. The key administrative issue here is to develop the institutional capacity—within Ministries of Environment as well as of Ministries of Finance—to understand the various linkages between economic policies and the environment.

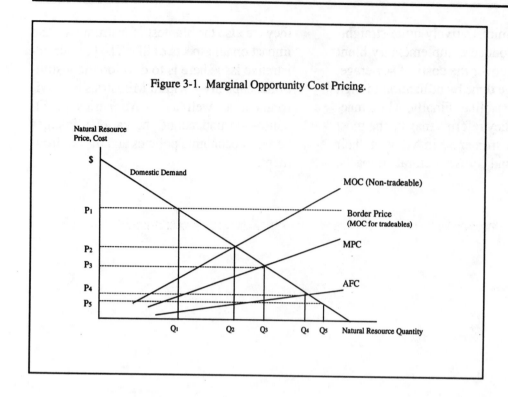

Figure 3-1. Marginal Opportunity Cost Pricing.

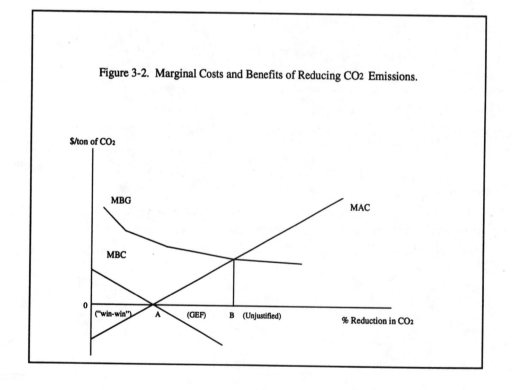

Figure 3-2. Marginal Costs and Benefits of Reducing CO_2 Emissions.

4

Macroeconomic Policy
and the Adjustment Process

AS WE HAVE NOTED, ENVIRONMENTAL DEGRADATION appears to
be an increasing threat to sustainable economic growth and
development, and therefore assumes macroeconomic proportions. At the same time, the impacts of policies at the macroeconomic level appear to be of major significance. In short, the
environment is no longer to be thought of as something distinct
from economics; indeed it should be central to it. This does not
merely imply concern at the project or sector level, but arguably
even more importantly, at the macroeconomic level.

National Income Accounting

The general principles now accepted as part of the "new" environmental economics recognize the environment as integral to development policy, but much still needs to be done to refine understanding of the macroeconomic importance of environmental problems, and in particular to be able to assess the extent to which economic growth is likely to be sustainable. The shortcomings of national income accounts in the treatment of the environment are now fairly well known. (See Box 4–1.) Pollution abatement or mitigation costs—for example, cleaning up after an oil spill—are counted as additions to national income. Of special relevance to many developing countries is that there is typically no accounting for the drawing down of the stock of those resources that, in principle, are renewable, but which in practice, because of overexploitation, are rapidly depleting. If compensating investment is not made, growth based on such a process is not sustainable, and conventional national income measures provide a misleadingly favorable impression of economic progress.

It has been suggested that treating natural capital depletion in a similar manner to depreciation of human-made capital would provide a more realistic indicator of economic progress. Indeed, environmental accounting studies have been completed for a number of developing countries, as well as for certain industrial countries.[1] These exercises are aimed at creating an awareness of environmental issues at the macroeconomic level and to identify sustainable development strategies. There are, however, arguments against reforming accounts in this way. To do so could lull policymakers into a false sense of security, since many of the most significant environmental issues are not susceptible to measurement in monetary terms. Moreover, national income accounts are basically indicators of the volume of economic activity. They are deficient in many respects as an indicator of human welfare, and adjusting for one deficiency—major though it is—does not change this. Nevertheless, development of a parallel set of physical resource accounts would undoubtedly be an important adjunct to conventional national income accounts.

Recent work on the treatment of environment in national income accounts has, however, highlighted one critical aspect of the relationship between economic policy and the environment. Virtually all definitions of "sustainable development" imply the need to pass on a stock of capital to future generations at least equal to that available for the use of the present generation. It is now widely accepted that "genuine savings" must be positive: in turn, this requires that the sum of natural and man-made capital must be maintained intact, or indeed, increased in real terms, if economic growth is to be continued into the future.[2]

Adjustment and the Environment

In recent years, changes in macroeconomic policies in the developing world have generally been associated with the process known as adjustment. While in principle, the adjustment process is merely a special case of macroeconomic policy change, in practice it is sufficiently important to use adjustment as a proxy for macroeconomic policy reform in analyzing the consequences for the environment, at this level of decisionmaking. Indeed, most of the analytical studies and virtually all the polemical ones on this subject have concentrated on adjustment rather than on macroeconomic policy in general.

Adjustment-related reforms have wide-ranging effects on economic incentives, and this has been recognized in a growing literature on their impacts on sectors of the econ-

[1]Repetto et al. 1989; Solorzano et al. 1991; Cruz and Repetto 1992.

[2]Pearce et al. 1993.

Box 4–1: Environmental Accounting

Economic performance is generally measured by the growth in gross domestic product (GDP). While GDP is a fairly accurate measure of market activity, it does not reflect the depletion of natural resource stocks and the degradation of the environment which often are not valued by the market. Lutz and Munasinghe (1991) identify three specific shortcomings in the current framework:

Natural and environmental resources are not fully included in balance sheets. National accounts represent limited indicators of public well-being since they do not have the capacity to measure changes in environmental and natural resource conditions.

Conventional national accounts fail to record the true costs of using natural resources in economic activity. The depletion or degradation of natural capital, which occurs in the course of productive activity (for example, through mining, fishing, or use of water) is not included in terms of current costs or depreciation of natural wealth. This leads to underestimation of the market value of resource-based goods—the lower the value added, the larger is the extent of underpricing of the final product (Dasgupta and Mäler 1990). Also, there are no estimates of the "hidden costs" associated with the export of primary products, suggesting that the contribution of the external sector in many developing countries is overestimated.

Cleanup or abatement activities (for example, those that result in expenditures incurred to restore environmental assets) often result in overestimation of the national income because the offsetting environmental damages are not considered. For example, losses from environmental damage are not included from national income accounting. However, when damage occurs, cleanup or restoration costs serve to increase the measures of income.

The deficiencies in the accounting techniques employed at present have suggested the need for a system of national accounts which permit the computation of an environmentally adjusted net domestic product and an environmentally adjusted net income. It has been proposed that a supplementary environmentally adjusted System of National Accounts (SNA) and corresponding performance indicators would encourage the reassessment of macroeconomic policies in light of environmental concerns and would help to trace the links between economywide policies and natural resource management (Muzondo and Miranda 1991).

---

omy that were not the original objects of the reform programs. The initial focus of this literature was on the social aspects of adjustment (Cornia, Jolly, and Stewart (eds.) 1987), but concern for the environmental implications of adjustment soon followed.

Although generally aimed at achieving macroeconomic stability and reducing domestic and foreign debt, the side effects of adjustment on the environment may be considerable, and take a variety of forms. These include changes in incentives governing resource use and conservation which may stem from economic reforms affecting the relative prices of macroeconomic or sectoral variables. Included in this category is pricing resources in accordance with full economic costs, removal or reduction of subsidies for agricultural and industrial inputs, and reduction in trade barriers. These changes may also stem from institutional reforms, such as the privatization of public enterprises, the distribution of forest concessions, or the promotion of land titling.

Many of these sector-specific reforms (of the kind discussed in the previous chapter) are in fact commonly found in sector adjustment operations, as noted below. Resource use, and therefore the environment, may also be affected via the income distributional consequences of adjustment measures. These include reforms aimed at reducing aggregate demand, with special focus on public expenditures in key economic sectors such as agriculture/forestry, energy, and industry, or, more typically, the social sectors (education and health).

The linkages between economic policy and the environment become increasingly complex the higher the level of decisionmaking, and the more pervasive the effects of changes in policy. This is exemplified by the various routes by which economic policy impacts upon incentives at the sector level, as illustrated in the previous chapter. The adjustment process, therefore, might be expected to exert an even more circuitous influence upon resource use, and therefore, by definition, upon the environment. This is consistent with findings regarding the influence of the macroeconomic context for agriculture, as shown by the classic studies of Johnson (1973) and Schuh (1974). More recently Krueger, Schiff, and Valdes (1991) have compiled detailed country examples suggesting that economy-wide factors may in fact be more important than sectoral policies in agriculture. These studies point out that when a broader assessment perspective is adopted, direct output price interventions by government often have less effect on agricultural incentives than indirect, economywide factors, such as foreign exchange rates and industrial protection policies.

Some of the complexities in identifying relationships between economic policies and the environment are illustrated in Table 4–1, the first column of which lists a number of strategic policy areas. The policy reforms in the second column are usually designed to address these issues, with the specific economic development objectives or direct impacts in the third column. Examples of second-order, unanticipated impacts are listed in the last column. It will be noted that the environmental effects could be either positive or negative. To properly evaluate such reforms, therefore, possible tradeoffs between their contribution to conventional development objectives and their environmental effects will need to be assessed. Relevant modifications—to prevent or reduce negative effects or to augment potential environmental benefits—can then be analyzed for each policy.

In a country specific context, a more detailed matrix based on Table 4–1 would be very useful from the viewpoint of macroeconomic and sectoral decisionmakers, especially those involved in national economic planning in the ministry of finance, ministry of planning, or key sectoral ministries. For them, the crucial question is how a specific economic policy—such as devaluation, price liberaliza-tion, reduction of government subsidies, or energy pricing reforms—will affect a range of environmental issues.

The results would also be useful from the viewpoint of environmental policymakers, such as officials charged with preparing the national environmental action plans. For them, the key question is which of a bewilderingly wide range of economic policies (current or proposed) would substantially affect a high-priority environmental issue. Certain types of policies can be expected to exert an impact upon particular environmental issues (Table 4–2). For example, if air pollution is a major concern, then the relevant policy would involve energy prices; for deforestation, foreign exchange and agricultural price policies; for water availability and quality, domestic price policies; and for energy efficiency, trade and exchange rate policies that influence international fuel prices. However, while there is reasonable consensus that relationships exist, their precise nature and even their direction is usually much less clear.

General Equilibrium Approaches

Ideally, the impact of the adjustment process on the environment would be addressed by considering not only the immediate, first round effects, but the subsequent consequences of feedbacks. In short, a general equilibrium approach would be desirable. Indeed, the systems effects that characterize relationships between economics and the environment has prompted a growing interest in the use of computable general equilibrium (CGE) models which attempt to take account of both behavioral and physical variables. CGE models can be useful by capturing the market failures which lead to environmental problems, thereby providing policymakers with an indication of the direct and indirect effects of their policies. Additionally, they might help to provide the structure within which national income accounting and environmentally aware policy analysis could be performed.

Early applications of CGE models to environmental concerns were undertaken in industrial countries. Alfsen, Glomsrod, and Hanson (1987) incorporated environmental components in a multisectoral growth model of Norway. The Central Bureau of Statistics of Norway has also used a CGE model in conjunction with an emissions forecasting model. Various types of emissions are analyzed (e.g., carbon dioxide, sulfuric oxide), together with four processes: stationary combustion, mobile combustion, process, evaporation. In this modeling work, the CGE model is run and then the environmental impacts are calculated.

Other modeling work in developed countries include a study on energy and economic growth in Sweden by Lars Bergman (1989). Sherman Robinson (1990) constructed a CGE model with an explicit pollution component, but utilized only hypothetical data. The approach included putting pollution and abatement results from the CGE model into a social welfare function, which was then optimized in a nonlinear programming model (with the CGE equations serving as the constraints).

CGE models have been increasingly used over the last fifteen years in addressing problems in developing countries. Recently, their applicability to environmental concerns has also been explored. An early application was by Cruz and Repetto (1992), which described how postwar government policies in the Philippines penalized lowland agriculture and subsidized an increasingly inefficient industrial sector. As a result, and compounded by rapid population growth, rural poverty worsened and the capacity of the economy to absorb a rapidly growing labor supply severely lagged. The onset of the economic crisis in the early 1980s and the contractionary nature of the stabilization policies intensified poverty and unemployment. The lack of livelihood opportunities in lowland agriculture and industry stimulated to the migration uplands, accelerating the deforestation of upper watersheds.

Neoclassical macroeconomic models usually incorporate capital and labor inputs in production sectors, generally ignoring the role of natural resources. In the Philippine CGE model, land inputs were included to allow an assessment of land use changes associated with policy reforms. Simulations with the model concluded that reforms to improve access to agricultural lands could contribute to reducing population pressures on forest lands by increasing labor absorption in lowland farms. Other simulations indicated that domestic resource mobilization based on increasing resource rent and energy taxes could lead to significant "win-win" outcomes. This could reduce the balance-of-payments deficit and expand employment, while controlling environmental degradation.

Another early modeling effort was undertaken by Panayotou and Sussangkarn (1991) for Thailand. This utilized a ninety-sector CGE macroeconomic model, using as a database a Social Accounting Matrix (SAM) of the Thai economy. Five structural adjustment-type policies were simulated, namely a reduction in export taxes on rice and rubber; an increase in domestic oil prices; an increase in labor-intensive manufactured export growth trend; an increase in tourism growth trend; and a reduction in real public sector investment.

The authors estimated that the increase in agricultural production that would result from a reduction in export taxes, would lead to (a) intensification of rice production and hence increased use of agro-chemicals; switching of land from upland crops to rice as well as increased investment in land improvement and soil conservation; and (b) extensification of rubber cultivation onto higher slopes and consequent deforestation and soil erosion. The increase in domestic oil prices would cause GDP to decline in all sectors, but there would be a reduction of energy-related emissions due to energy efficiency and conservation, and a shift at the margin from more energy-intensive to less energy-intensive activities.

The increase in labor-intensive manufactured growth trend would have both negative and positive environmental impacts. Labor-intensive industries tend to be more intensive in local natural resources, and may intensify depletion. Some labor-intensive industries such as tanneries and slaughterhouses would lead to increased water pollution. As labor is attracted out of services, an increase in wastes and emissions may occur. However, attracting labor out of agriculture could lead to reduced deforestation rates, and a move away from heavy industry would reduce atmospheric pollution. For the most part, increased tourism would lead to destruction of coastal lands, and an increase in marine and air pollution (through increased energy use). However, a shift to less erosive high-value crops such as fruit and vegetables would be environmentally beneficial. The model indicated that the environmental impact of a reduction in real public sector investments would be an increase in natural resource depletion, forest encroachment and agricultural pollution. There would be a reduction in urban and industrial pollution since these sectors would shrink.

The quantitative results of this exercise clearly should be interpreted with great care. Data problems are pervasive, not least because much of the data went back to 1984. Since then there has been a period of extremely rapid economic growth in Thailand, during which all parameters have doubtless changed significantly. However, this important effort highlights the kind of information needed to be able to anticipate with any accuracy the environmental consequences of policy reform.

Of particular relevance for our purpose, however, is that in the Philippines and Thailand studies the parameters linking economic variables and their environmental impacts, as well as the economic impacts of environmental change were not integrated into the macroeconomic model. The difficulty of generating the data needed for explicitly incorporating environmental processes in CGE models suggests that the priority now is to develop

better partial equilibrium models. These will serve as the building blocks required for improved understanding of economy-environment linkages. In other words, a general equilibrium *approach*, based upon partial equilibrium *models*, is, given the state of the art and the lack of information, the appropriate strategy in most countries.

In the case studies described in Volume II, the Costa Rica and Morocco studies do apply a CGE modeling approach, but most of the other studies done to date use a partial equilibrium approach. The ones that are mentioned below also tend to emphasize certain aspects of the adjustment process or macroeconomic policy on the environment, most of them being restricted to a particular sector or subsector, and addressing a specific determinant of environmental behavior, such as institutional factors, poverty and income distribution, or debt and trade issues.

Institutional Aspects of Economic Reforms

A number of studies have attempted to trace through the effects of the adjustment process at the sector level, emphasizing the importance of institutional factors. One of the earliest was a study of policy reform and natural resource management in Sub-Saharan Africa (Stryker et al. 1989). The study evaluated the stabilization and structural adjustment programs adopted by Sudan in 1978, with respect to implications for deforestation. The structural adjustment program included the liberalization of foreign exchange transactions and a devaluation of the exchange rate. These were combined with other measures such as the removal of price controls and the removal of consumer subsidies and were aimed at increasing production of cash crops (particularly cotton).

The study considered various implications of these reforms on forest resources. The first effect would be land clearing and this would directly result in forest depletion. Second, if crops such as cotton were grown without adequate fertilization, soil erosion and fertility depletion would increase, thereby adding to the problems caused by deforestation. Third, the removal of subsidies on petroleum would lead to increased demand for wood as fuel substitutes, limiting the effectiveness of policies to protect forested areas. Finally, cuts in government expenditure were expected to reduce funding of forest protection and reforestation programs.

The authors do not arrive at definitive conclusions about the impacts of these policies that result from structural adjustment programs. However, they support implementation of direct measures being pursued by the Sudanese Government to address the potential environmental problem. Within the forestry sector itself, these measures include restricting the rate of commercial exploitation and encouraging replanting and agro-forestry. With respect to the intersectoral fuel aspect, they propose government-sponsored programs to improve the allocation of fuel supplies.

The study also looked at the reform process in Senegal and the implications for irrigation management. In this case, it was expected that the shift in decisionmaking towards a greater role for irrigation associations and individual farmers, would improve irrigation management, and limit problems of oversalinity and waterlogging caused by current practices.

In Nigeria, the study considered the potential environmental impacts of the structural adjustment program undertaken in 1986. The policy reforms—currency devaluation and trade liberalization—were associated with increased prices of most agricultural products, in particular internationally tradeable ones. Most subsidies were removed. Although fertilizer subsidies were retained, budgetary constraints did not allow for adequate financing, and market prices rose steeply. Small farmers were affected the most. Nevertheless, the authors conclude that the reforms will have a positive impact overall as farmers will be encouraged to invest in soil conservation

practices as a response to higher prices.

It is clear from Stryker's work that while price-related changes are of great significance, they do not work in a vacuum. Their eventual impact depends upon a host of other factors, not least of which is the institutional structure within which they operate. Examples include the problems caused by insecurity of land tenure which reduces the incentives for resource conservation, or inequitable access to land, which worsens population pressure on marginal resources, leading to deforestation and soil erosion.

The direction of changes in resource use will depend to a large extent on the nature of intervening institutional factors. Thus, there is no simple relationship between price-related policy reforms and the environment. For example, if potential economic returns from crops increase, this will lead to increased cropping activity and therefore more land exploitation. The implication for land conservation, however, will be very different, depending on whether croplands are protected by secure rights or not. In the first case, increased potential returns may lead to parallel investment in the land resource. However, in the second case, improved crop prices will result in "mining" the land resource or in opening up new lands for cultivation, regardless of the implication for declining productivity.

A number of other studies have recognized the environmental relevance of institutional factors, an important example being the work of Perrings et al. (1988) on the problem of overgrazing in Botswana. This study demonstrates that the lack of clearly defined property rights resulted in individual herders putting as many cattle as possible on the range, leading to overgrazing, bush encroachment, erosion and local desertification.

Cruz and Gibbs (1990) analyze the problem of population pressure on forest lands in the Philippines and Nepal. They propose that lack of secure property rights and the presence of substantial population pressure on marginal resources require that policy reform efforts should also attempt to modify the rules governing access to and use of natural resources.

Development agencies have also increasingly been challenged to respond to the need for institutional reform in the interest of environmental goals (Holmberg 1991). A study by the United Nations Economic Commission for Latin America and the Caribbean (ECLAC) focused on the role of land concentration issues and the environmental implications of the debt crisis in Latin America (ECLAC 1989). In this study, concentration of agricultural land is identified as a factor leading to income inequality and pressure on marginal resources, even in areas where physical population densities are not excessively high.

Other studies have recognized how institutional factors can interact with the effects of price changes. For example, open-access overexploitation of fishery resources results from the absence of property rights that allows anyone to harvest the resource. Since individual resource users cannot benefit from conserving such open access resources, the rational choice is to harvest as long as average returns from fishing are positive. This same overfishing situation will result even if there were secure fishing rights, if discount rates are extremely high (Clark 1976). In Cote d'Ivoire, the effects of government pricing policies were believed to have led to deforestation, but to a lesser extent than the lack of a consistent and secure land tenure system (Reed (ed.) 1992).

Lopez (1991) directly addresses the interaction between the effects of price changes and the institutional factors governing resource ownership and management in Cote d'Ivoire. Using both household economic data and remote sensing information on agricultural and forest resources, Lopez finds that increased output prices may contribute to pressures for agricultural extensification. However, if producers have secure tenure and can internalize the implications of excessive resource exploitation, these pressures can be significantly reduced.

An early study of Thailand illustrated the importance of complementary measures to ensure that successful economic growth policies do not conflict with environmental objectives.[3] For example, in the absence of clear delineation of property rights, increased incentives induced farmers to overexploit fragile lands; while industrial growth, unaccompanied by adequate regulatory or economic instruments, was associated with major environmental damage. Although the quantitative results of this exercise should be interpreted with care (because of data constraints), they make a useful contribution and, in agreement with others, highlight the kind of information needed to be able to anticipate with greater accuracy, the environmental consequences of policy reform.[4]

Finally, institutional change at its most dramatic—involving massive changes in the whole system of incentives countrywide—is currently under way in both Eastern Europe and China. As the above studies suggest, the assessment of the impact of economic incentives in isolation from institutional change—or vice versa—would be a totally artificial exercise.

Income Distribution, Poverty, and the Environment

Two specific distributional concerns have arisen with regard to the adjustment process. The first focuses on the decline of environmental services associated with the government spending cuts mandated by many stabilization and adjustment programs. The second deals with the more general relationships between adjustment reforms and their impact on poverty and the environment.

The early view of the environmental implications of the distributive impacts of adjustment-related reforms paralleled con-

---

[3]Panayotou and Sussangkarn 1991.

[4]Devarajan 1990; Robinson 1990.

cerns raised about the social impacts of adjustment. Since the 1970s, the redistribution of wealth and the recognition of the importance of fulfilling basic human needs, was given increasing currency among international development agencies, and reflected in *World Development Report 1980.*[5] The 1960s emphasis on economic growth as the key to development and poverty reduction had given way to the view that more direct poverty programs and investments in human resources were crucial in any attempts to address poverty.[6]

Concern with the social aspects of adjustment was motivated by the apprehension that adjustment programs being implemented by the IMF and the World Bank would revert to a growth focus, at the expense of distributional objectives. Its predominant focus was how reform programs had failed to protect social expenditures as fiscal austerity was imposed to stabilize the economy. This meant that the poor, who would be most vulnerable to the effects of macroeconomic contraction, would also be deprived of "safety nets" as social services were cut.

Similarly, the early adjustment and environment literature focused on cuts in government spending and their implications on environmental protection services. For example, a study undertaken by ECLAC (1989) concluded that adjustment policies pursued in Latin America in the 1980s led to cutbacks in current expenditure allotments for managing and supervising investment in sectors such as energy, irrigation, infrastructure, and mining. This limited the funds available for environmental impact assessments and the supervision of projects to control their environmental impacts. Muzondo and Miranda (1991), in an IMF survey, recognized this problem and suggested that high levels of government expenditure in other areas had led to reduced

funding of environmental activities. Recent case studies attributed increases in air pollution problems in Thailand and Mexico to reductions in expenditures for adequate infrastructure (Reed (ed.) 1992).

While the argument that government cutbacks undertaken as part of adjustment austerity efforts may undermine the funding for environmental initiatives sounds a reasonable one, empirical assessment of its actual importance is difficult. Decomposing government expenditures to shed light on what constitutes environmental activities is not feasible without a major data-gathering and interpretation exercise. In one effort that was undertaken to assess the social consequences of adjustment lending in Africa, it was found that although there have been declines in government expenditures, the budget proportion going to social expenditures and agriculture actually increased during the adjustment period.[7]

The results of studies focusing on social safety nets during adjustment programs confirm that pursuing fiscal discipline and macroeconomic stability need not take place at the cost of increased hardship for the poor. In much the same way, specific environmental concerns can be incorporated in stabilization efforts. For example, it has been reported that in many countries in Sub-Saharan Africa, forestry departments and their activities have always been severely underfunded.[8] Thus, targeted efforts to support forestry management activities could, with reasonable cost, be included in reform packages as part of a proactive environmental response. In brief, both critical environmental and social expenditures could be protected if government budget cuts are made judiciously.

Emphasis has recently shifted to another mechanism through which distributive policies might affect the environment. Thus, widespread poverty in conjunction with rapid

---

[5]World Bank 1980.

[6]See Cornia, Jolly, and Stewart (eds.) 1987.

[7]World Bank 1994a.

[8]Stryker et al. 1989.

population growth has been linked to increasing pressure on marginal agricultural resources. (See Box 4–2, Poverty and the Environment.) For example, Cleaver and Schreiber (1991) identify this poverty, population, and agricultural extensification nexus as the critical environmental challenge for Sub-Saharan Africa. Since unemployment and poverty may be exacerbated by short-term contractionary effects of stabilization programs, there will correspondingly be important implications for population pressure on marginal resources. Moreover, Cruz and Gibbs, as noted above, also show that in addition to inadequate economic policies, poverty, population growth, and institutional factors all conspire to threaten sustainable environmental management in the Philippines.

Debt and the environment

The issue of high levels of debt (often associated with sustained periods of government budget deficits, and macroeconomic instability) and its implications for environmental degradation have frequently been raised. For example, the Brundtland Report (WCED 1987) noted that: *debt that cannot be amortized forces raw material-dependent countries in Africa to deplete their fragile soils, with the result that good land is turned into desert.* The perception was that many countries reacted to the external shocks during the economic crisis years of the early 1980s by exploiting natural resources unsustainably. However, evidence from country case studies and from cross-country statistical exercises does not support this view.

For example, a World Wildlife Fund report, based on case studies for Cote d'Ivoire, Mexico, and Thailand, conclude the there is no simple relationship between external debt levels and environmental degradation. In the case of Cote d'Ivoire the research team found that although the country's deforestation rate was one of the highest in the world, external debt did not affect environmental degradation in general or the forestry sector in particular

(Reed (ed.) 1992). In another study, using econometric models with cross-country deforestation data, no consistent statistical relationship was found between debt and forest depletion (Capistrano and Kiker 1990).

In fact, many factors are at work, and primary commodities such as timber exports do not exhibit any simple trend during the debt crisis and adjustment periods. For example, in the early 1980s, primary commodity exports were subject to falling international commodity prices. Thus, production, domestic absorption, and price effects need to be assessed for specific commodities and countries (Reisen and Van Trotsenburg 1988). Indeed, since the debt crisis was associated with falling export prices and domestic economic contraction for many developing countries, it would not be unreasonable to expect that in some countries the rate of resource extraction, instead of increasing, would have actually declined during this period. Ultimately, what really matters is what debt is used for. Ideally, countries go into debt with the expectation that the benefits from the productive activities to be funded will more than pay for the loan. In practice, projects that are funded by external debt may be unsuccessful. Worse the capital may be diverted to other uses, and the country is left with accumulated debt, and little economic improvement to show for it. In the environmental context, debt-for-nature projects represent an effort to directly channel debt (or in this case its converse, debt relief) to beneficial environmental activities. In countries, such as Costa Rica, debt relief programs have allowed environmental agencies to fund forest or biodiversity protection initiatives.

Hansen (1990) has also questioned the direct link proposed between natural resource degradation, specifically deforestation, and the debt crisis. Employing basic macroeconomic analysis, Hansen points out that capital imports could include technological improvements that would enable better management of the resource base, as easily as they could lead

---

Box 4–2: Poverty and the Environment

The struggle to overcome poverty, daunting in itself is made more difficult in the face of increasingly apparent environmental constraints. A critical question for policymakers thus becomes whether the environmental aspects of poverty can be alleviated by modifying existing approaches, or if a wholly new strategy is required. A brief look at what is known about the reinforcing interplay of poverty and environmental degradation provides some clues.

The Environment's Impact on the Poor

Health problems. The poor are the most vulnerable in terms of exposure to certain types of pollution, such as unclean water that carries infectious and parasitic diseases. They (especially women and children) also suffer disproportionately from indoor air pollution that results from burning unclean, but accessible, bio-fuels. For example, smoke in household kitchens in poor rural areas of The Gambia, India, Kenya, and Nepal routinely have suspended particulate matter concentrations exceeding World Health Organization peak guidelines by four to five times.

Lower productivity. Environmental degradation depresses the poor's income by diverting more time to routine household tasks such as fuelwood collection and by decreasing the productivity of the natural resources from which the rural poor are most likely to wrest a living. A study of Nepalese hill villages with severe deforestation concluded that time devoted to fuelwood collection was diverting nearly a quarter of household labor normally devoted to agricultural activities, resulting in income loss and declining consumption and nutrition levels.

How Poverty Affects the Environment

Constrained time horizons. The very poor, struggling at subsistence levels of consumption and preoccupied with day-to-day survival, have limited scope to plan ahead and make natural resource investments (for example, soil conservation) that give positive returns only after a number of years. Such short time horizons are not innate characteristics, but rather the outcome of policy, institutional, and social failures.

Constrained risk strategies. The poor's use of natural resources is affected by their facing greater risks, with fewer means to cope. These risks range from misguided policy interventions in input and output markets to evolving land tenure systems that favor those with greater political clout. The rich array of traditional means for coping with crises—selling stored crops or goods, migration of household members, increasing wage labor, borrowing for consumption, calling on mutual assistance traditions or patron-client understandings—are often unavailable to the poor or are weakening as social norms. This means that the poor will have little choice but to overexploit any available natural resources. Moreover, the poor, especially the women, typically lack access to formal markets for credit, crop insurance, and information (for example, extension services) that provide advice on risk-reducing agricultural practices.

Source: Mink 1993.

---

to further exploitation of the natural resource base. He concludes that unless there were a shift in domestic production to the forestry sector as a result of debt-servicing, or a shift to a more hazardous forest extraction technology, there would be no automatic increase in deforestation because of the debt crisis.

Regarding debt-for-nature campaigns, one of the most successful applications of this strategy was in Costa Rica, where the government managed to purchase about US$70 million of debt (5 percent of its commercial debt) from debt-for-nature grants (World Resources Institute 1989). However, this amount was exceptionally large because of the unusual worldwide interest in Costa Rica's forestry and biodiversity resources, and the process is probably not replicable in most indebted countries. It also has been noted that some awareness-raising gains might follow from such debt-for-nature campaigns (Pearce and Warford 1993). However, such efforts may not make any significant dent in the level of outstanding debts for most countries. Furthermore, the process does not directly address the critical need for policy and institutional reforms in the resource and environmental sector.

To directly address the policy relevance issue, Cruz and Repetto (1992) have proposed the more general link: debt, deficits, and resource degradation are all forms of asset decline or increased liability, leading to deterioration of future income to maintain current consumption. Economywide policies and incentive distortions, motivated by myopic macroeconomic objectives, are the common determinants of this process of declining national wealth.

This perspective is consistent with the observed correlation between debt and degradation. More importantly it leads to fruitful prescriptions for macroeconomic policy reforms. For example, resource accounts for the Philippines demonstrate a general decline in resource assets during the 1970s and 1980s. This was associated with the shortfall in savings, low returns on investments, and the continued increase in external indebtedness that shifted resources to current uses at the expense of future income. Tariff and exchange rate policies encouraged resource extraction and disinvestment in the primary production sector, thereby reducing the sustainable yield from the resource stock. Thus, macroeconomic policy variables are explicitly identified and linked to the general problem of myopic economic management and the specific problems of increasing national liabilities (from debt) and decreasing assets (from degradation).

Developing such policy relevant approaches will require more research, especially in terms of constructing models and testing these against specific country experiences. These efforts need to be coordinated with studies that are also being undertaken in several countries on two related themes. The first refers to natural resource accounting. As noted earlier, to comprehend macroeconomic trends in resource decline there is a need for a macroeconomic measure of resource degradation. Secondly, research on macroeconomic policy-environment links also have to build on the results of studies that evaluate resource- or sector-specific distortions that encourage overexploitation. There should be better recognition that macroeconomic reforms are being introduced and are affecting resource use decisions in a context where there are long-standing incentive distortions. Clearly, the impact of reform programs that alter macroeconomic prices will also be contingent on existing distortions at the sector level.

Trade and environment

As noted by the 1992 *World Development Report* on development and the environment (World Bank 1992k), the concern with environmental implications of trade involves both the domestic implications of policy reforms as well as the global environmental dimension of international trade agreements. Although liberalizing reforms generally promote more efficient resource use (including use of environmental resources), in practice there is no clear-cut reason to expect that trade liberalization will be either good or bad for the environment. The reason is that trade reforms may be undertaken, but the presence of pre-existing market, policy or institutional imperfections in the environment sector may lead to adverse environmental impacts. The following discussion illustrates various environmental initiatives that will be needed to complement reforms in the trade sector.

Regarding national or domestic trade reforms, early concerns about negative effects were raised regarding the North American Free Trade Agreement (NAFTA) and pollution in Mexico. Similar concerns involved cassava exports and soil erosion in Thailand, and exchange rate depreciation and deforestation in Ghana. However, more recently there has been increased recognition that the links between trade and the environment are much more complex since economic expansion from trade is characterized not only by growth but also by changes in the intersectoral composition of output, in production techniques and input use, and in location of economic activity.

For example, if liberalized trade fosters greater efficiency and higher productivity, it may also reduce pollution intensity by encouraging the growth of less polluting industries and the adoption of cleaner technologies. In Mexico, Grossman and Krueger (1991) conclude that increased specialization due to NAFTA-related trade liberalization would result in a shift to labor-intensive and agricultural activities that require less energy inputs and generate less hazardous waste per unit of output than more capital-intensive activities. Similarly, in the Indonesia case study (Volume II), both pollution and energy intensity declined due to such shifts. Pollution impacts probably declined as well, due to the dispersion of industry away from Java. However, the rapid growth of the industrial sector in recent years has also meant an increase in total pollution in spite of reduced pollution intensities. This needs to be addressed aggressively with a combination of regulations and economic incentives.

On agriculture and forestry, contrary to popular perceptions, a shift in cropping patterns towards export crops expansion does not necessarily imply increased erosion. Repetto (1989), using examples for Sub-Saharan Africa, concludes that many export crops tend to be less harmful to soils. In West Africa, tree and bush crops are grown with grasses, and erosion rates are 2–3 times less than similar areas planted for locally used food crops such as cassava, yams, maize, sorghum, and millet. In Malawi, Cromwell and Winpenny (1991) found that adjustment led to changes in product mix and production intensity instead of changes in cultivated area or production techniques. Soil improving crops were adopted and agricultural intensification helped absorb a rapidly growing population on less land. Also, contrary to popular belief, export crop expansion has not generally occurred at the cost of reduced food crop output, with subsequent potentially negative social and environmental effects. However, in a study of 11 developing countries, it was found that rapid

expansion of cash crops, in fact, does not tend to reduce food production (Braun and Kennedy 1986). This complementarity rather than competition has been observed in countries where initial productivity is low and is partly explained by technology spillovers from cash crop activities that also enhance food crop production.

The more pressing question is whether these export crops displace forests. In Sudan, Stryker et al. (1989) found that trade and other adjustment-related reforms resulted in significant deforestation because increased producer prices encouraged woodland clearing for crop cultivation. However, recent studies have shown that in such cases, deforestation pressures are due to prevailing distortions within the forestry sector, such as very low stumpage prices or poor forest management capacity that are not corrected with the trade reforms. Inadequate land tenure and land clearing as a requirement for tenure, prevent more efficient exploitation of existing agricultural lands, and have also contributed to the problem. For example, in Cote d'Ivoire, the effects of price-related policies were believed to have led to deforestation, but to a lesser extent than the lack of a consistent and secure land tenure system (Reed (ed.) 1992). The Ghana study also analyzed the interaction between effects of price changes and the institutional factors governing resource ownership and management. Using both household data and remote sensing information on agricultural and forest resources, the study found that increased crop incentives have contributed to pressures for deforestation. However, if producers had secure tenure and could internalize the implications of excessive land exploitation, these pressures would have been reduced significantly.[9]

With regard to the global environmental dimension of international trade, the debate has revolved around the issue of whether freer trade is beneficial to global and national

---

[9]See the Ghana case study in Volume II.

environmental conditions and whether it should be used to influence national and international environmental standards and agreements. Studies arising from a recent General Agreement on Tariffs and Trade (GATT) symposium have concluded that expanding global production and consumption does not necessarily cause greater environmental degradation (Anderson and Blackhurst 1992). Indeed, with appropriate national policy reforms greater trade would generally contribute to environmental gains. In the case of coal, trade liberalization and the removal of price supports in richer countries would reduce coal output, lead to higher international prices, and consequently decrease coal consumption. This would be beneficial for the environment. In the case of food production, the reduction of agricultural trade protection in rich countries would lead to a relocation of production to poorer countries, leading to greater incomes, and reduced agricultural pollution in developed countries. In poorer countries, it is recognized that the incentive to produce more will probably increase fertilizer and pesticide use. However, maintaining high levels of agricultural protection in rich countries is an inefficient way of protecting the environment.

Domestic tax incentives and regulations would be a better way of limiting environmental degradation. (Anderson and Blackhurst 1992; Lutz 1992). The same general conclusion is reached in recent studies on biodiversity and forestry. For example, the overexploitation of biodiversity and wildlife for international trade plays a minor role in species extinction since the major cause is habitat destruction (Burgess 1991). Thus, attempts to ban wildlife trade will have limited benefit plus large cost; proper trade mechanisms such as taxes and subsidies would be better at encouraging conservation. With respect to global deforestation, Barbier et al. (1991) found that the timber trade has not been the major source of deforestation. The domestic factors (distorted prices, subsidies, tax re-

gimes, regulations, management capacity) leading to conversion of forest land to agriculture has played the larger role. In general, an appropriate combination of domestic environmental and agricultural policy measures, combined with trade reforms, will result in both welfare gains and in environmental quality (Harold and Runge 1993). On the international front, however, the challenge is to initiate coordinated international action on domestic reform measures that will counter the environmentally threatening scale effects, because any country attempting to implement domestic reforms in isolation will loose income and jobs to its neighbors.

On the effect of freer trade with different national environmental standards between North and South, an early view was that dirty industries would migrate to poor countries, where environmental standards were either less strict or nonexistent (Leonard (ed.) 1989). Recent work indicates that pollution abatement and control expenditures by firms do not appear to have had a significant effect on competitiveness in most industries since these expenditures represent a modest share of total costs. For example, environmental costs generally comprise only .5 percent of output value and only 3 percent for the most polluting industry (Low (ed.) 1993). Thus, environmental costs are not the dominating factor in decisions for locating new industrial investments. In fact, trade openness which may promote newer technologies may tend to have positive environmental effects since most new technologies are also cleaner (Birdsall and Wheeler 1992; Huq and Wheeler 1993).

These findings also suggest that there is no pressing reason for requiring national environmental standards to be made identical. Patterns of resource exploitation and pollution are primarily affected by economic and social conditions, with environmental regulations or standards (especially in poor countries) playing a minor role. Promoting acceptance of similar environmental principles, such as requiring that polluters pay for the damages

---

Box 4–3: Environmental Concerns and Adjustment Lending

For many years now, the World Bank has advocated integrating environmental concerns into economic reforms, and as a recent study shows, the rhetoric is being translated into action.

A review of Bank adjustment lending operations over the period FY88–FY92 found that about 60 percent of the sampled loans explicitly included environmental goals or loans conditionalities addressing environmental concerns in agriculture, forestry, energy, trade, and industry. This was up sharply from only 37 percent during the FY79–FY87 period. Moreover, the recent loans encompassed a much wider range of policy instruments or sectoral strategies (e.g., from energy and resource pricing reforms to institutional capacity building).

For the study, the Bank selected 81 loans, which represented about 65 percent of total adjustment lending during the FY88–FY92 period. This included 47 structural adjustment loans and 34 sectoral adjustment loans in 58 countries spread throughout the developing world. The rest of the loans were excluded, because they were mostly financial sector adjustment programs considered to have no direct—or traceable—implications for the environment.

One caveat, however: It is important to note that such lending operations have specific, fairly short-run objectives, and the loans are meant for rapid disbursement. While environmental objectives can, and increasingly are, built into loan conditions, there are many other environmental goals that require long-term institutional and capacity reform and for which adjustment lending is not an appropriate instrument.

Source: Warford et al. 1994.

---

they inflict or incorporating environmental values in cost-benefit analysis, will probably be more effective as well as politically more acceptable.

Further work in this field should include efforts to establish more clearly (a) the conditions leading to intensification as opposed to extensive land use at the agricultural frontier; (b) the extent to which pollution from industrial growth may undermine declining pollution intensity effects from trade reforms; and (c) whether trade measures should be resorted to as "second best" policies when international coordination on removal of domestic distortions fail.

World Bank Adjustment Lending Operations

The World Bank has for several years advocated the integration of environmental concerns in economic reforms as a key priority, and has made significant steps in building this into its own operations. A World Bank paper (Warford et al. 1994) examines the relationships between the adjustment process and the environment and, in particular, about the extent to which World Bank adjustment lending activities adequately address environ-

mental issues. The paper stresses that in addressing the linkages between adjustment lending and the environment, it is important to bear in mind that such lending operations have specific, fairly short-run objectives in mind, and the loans are intended for rapid disbursement. The following assessment indicates that while environmental objectives can, and increasingly are, built in to loan conditions, there are many other environmental objectives that require long-term institutional and capacity reform and for which adjustment lending is a singularly inappropriate instrument.

The adjustment process is facilitated not merely by adjustment lending operations, but also by the whole range of sector and project activities in which the Bank, other development agencies and, of course, the countries themselves are engaged. In fact, many of the policy reforms contained in the adjustment process—particularly in sector adjustment lending—are far from new. Reforms, such as rationalization of electricity pricing or removal of subsidies for pesticides, have been standard elements of project and sector lending for many years. Whether they have been related or not to adjustment lending, macroeconomic dialogue as well as lending and policy work in a variety of sectors—ranging from energy to population—may have profound impacts not only upon the adjustment process but also on the environment.

During the early to mid-1980s, environmental issues were limited considerations in adjustment lending, although there were often potential complementarities between adjustment policies and environmental objectives. In the last several years, by contrast, adjustment programs include more than just a nominal treatment of the environment. Environmental issues have become an important aspect in adjustment lending by the Bank. (Refer to Box 4–3.) There are now more adjustment loans with components or conditionalities that are openly environmentally motivated. Indeed, environmental programs have in some cases been the primary objective of adjustment operations.

This assessment of the evolution of adjustment is at odds with the criticism that adjustment operations ignore environmental concerns. On the contrary, adjustment is a necessary, if not sufficient, condition for sound environmental management. Certainly stability, "getting prices right," and public sector reform have virtually unambiguous—and beneficial—impacts on the environment. Trade reform, in enhancing efficiency and employing the principle of comparative advantage, will also tend to do so. In each case, however, there may be unanticipated effects, which require complementary or compensatory interventions. This might be especially apparent in the case of trade policy: encouraging exports, if not accompanied by adequate pricing or institutional policies in the country concerned, could lead to overexploitation of a natural resource, such as forest products. However, freer trade itself would not be the culprit, but failure to address the "second best" conditions prevailing elsewhere in the economy would be.

It is recognized that environmental problems and their solution tend to be location-specific and heavily dependent upon the prevailing culture and physical environment.

However, it is important that those responsible for economic and sectoral management should be aware of the nature of the linkages between these variables. They should be prepared to take appropriate measures either to use the leverage of such policies to bring about pervasive environmental improvement, or at least be prepared to take compensatory measures to avoid potentially adverse social or environmental consequences of those policies.

In conclusion, while critics may have been correct in the past about how the environment was not being systematically integrated into World Bank adjustment lending, that is certainly not true now. Even in the past, when there was limited concern over the environment, the resulting neglect was not necessarily bad. On the contrary, good economics, particularly as it emphasizes efficient use of resources, is often good for the environment too. As this review has stressed, there remain, due in large part to government policy failure, many opportunities for policies that satisfy both economic and environmental objectives. It should continue to be a primary strategic objective of individual countries as well as of development institutions such as the World Bank to search out such opportunities, and to give them priority in their investment programs, and institutional and economic policy measures.

Conclusion

Most of the work referred to in this chapter has focused on the relationship between specific adjustment-related reforms and the environment. This experience demonstrates that there is an important interface between economywide policies and the incentives governing natural resource use. However, more work needs to be done to weigh the implications of these links and to design effective policy modifications or alternatives. This will typically require a distinction to be made between (a) the short-term stabilization components and (b) the longer-term incentive modifying aspects of adjustment programs, since these categories of reform tend to differ in their environmental implications and therefore call for different remedial actions.

The short-term effects work primarily through the aggregate demand contraction associated with stabilization efforts. These effects may substantially differ from the effects of longer-term changes that modify production incentives for resource use and pollution. For example, a reduction in government expenditures or increased unemployment from contractionary policies may increase deforestation pressures through the poverty route. However, contractionary policies will also reduce domestic absorption and may therefore decrease deforestation from commercial logging. By contrast, reforming the structure of incentives may have longer-term implications for various sectoral activities that differ from the short-term effects. An example of these longer-term effects is how foreign exchange liberalization will generally expand the traded goods sector, thus encouraging resource-based exports such as timber.

The modifications to adjustment programs in response to the short-term negative environmental effects of stabilization are conceptually more straightforward—though not necessarily easier to implement. The contractionary effects of adjustment, although they can clearly increase unemployment and poverty, are sometimes justified on the argument that excessive inflation or loss of international credit are far more costly. However, there is growing recognition that unemployment and poverty can be directly addressed by targeted programs and changing the emphasis on stabilization instruments can additionally cushion indirect social costs. (See, for example, Blejer and Guerrero 1990.) Environmentally oriented modifications could mostly parallel these changes that have been proposed to reduce the short run social costs of adjustment.

The required response to the environmental implications of longer-term incentive changes are more complex. For these reforms sectoral or intersectoral issues, and in particular, the influence of site-specific physical, institutional and cultural variables, need to be explicitly considered. Adjustment programs, insofar as they advocate economywide reforms that remove distortions from inappropriate macroeconomic policies, are needed in many developing countries. However, when there are major environmental externalities involved or when sectoral government or institutional distortions exist for specific resources, it is not clear that better macroeconomic prices will lead to more efficient resource use. For example, in the case of forestry higher export prices from adjustment efforts couple with continuing sectoral timber underpricing constitute the main ingredients for more deforestation. This means that for this class of adjustment-environment linkages both macroeconomic reforms and sector-specific aspects will need to be considered.

While the studies and experience reviewed above tend to reinforce the general notion that economic policy is a potentially important tool to be used in environmental management, it also suggests that generalizations are difficult to make. What may appear to be identical policy reforms may have dramatically different impacts in different situations, depending on such things as the prevailing institutional arrangements, prices of other goods, and the physical and cultural environment.[10] Policy reforms that might intuitively be expected to be environmentally benign, may in fact have the opposite result. Increased prices of commercial energy might stimulate overuse of biomass and deforestation; reducing pesticide subsidies may also reduce the production of otherwise environmentally benign crops, and so on.

The evidence produced so far is fragmentary and incomplete, and it is necessary at this stage to produce more case material to illustrate the range and nature of the interrelationships between countrywide (macroeconomic

---

[10]World Bank 1989c.

or sectoral) policies and the environment. Such case material should involve more attention than in the past to the importance of other (noneconomic) variables influencing outcomes, as well as explicit attention to the policy choices. Thus, after all "no regrets" options have been exhausted, environmental measures may conflict with other legitimate objectives—growth, development, poverty alleviation—case studies are required in which economic policy and the environment are placed firmly in an overall development context.

Finally, it will be observed that this book does not consider the implications of growth itself for the environment. Clearly some improvement follows increased income per capita. However, there are reasons to doubt, as Herman Daly constantly reminds us, the feasibility of sustainable economic growth into the indefinite future.[11] The challenge of raising living standards, particularly in light of the high population growth rates in the poorest countries, is immense. So is the gap between rich and poor. The prospects for continued economic development will rest heavily upon human capacity to adapt to natural resource depletion, on technical progress, and the ability to substitute natural for human-made capital. A major challenge for economists is to develop strategies that smooth the transition to a sustainable society, by means of policies which satisfy both short-term economic objectives and which are also environmentally benign. Clearly, economic policy instruments will be indispensable means of restricting wasteful, environmentally destructive use of resources. In this sense, reconciling sound environmental management with economic adjustment is essential.

---

[11]See, for example, Daly and Cobb 1989.

Table 4–1: Critical Environmental Links for Economic Planners

Policy Issues	Policy Reforms	Direct Objectives/Effects	Indirect (Environmental) Effects
1. Trade deficits	Flexible exchange rates	Promote exports; reduce imports	Export promotion may lead to more deforestation for export, but it could also lead to substitution of tree crops for annual crops. In addition, industrial job creation may reduce pressures on land resources
2. Food security and unemployment	Agricultural intensification in settled lands and resettlement programs for new areas	Increase crop yields and acreage; absorb more rural labor	May reduce spontaneous migration to ecologically fragile areas. However, there is potential for overuse of fertilizers and chemicals
3. Lack of industrial competitiveness	Reduction of tariffs and special incentives	Promote competition and industrial efficiency	More openness may lead industry to adopt more energy-efficient or less pollution-prone technologies. However, it may also lead to influx of hazardous industries

Table 4–2: Critical Economic Policy Links for Environmental Planners

Resource / Environmental Management Issue	Sectoral Economic Characteristics	Relevant Policy Reforms
1. Agricultural expansion and deforestation	Many small, competitive decision-makers are involved	Reduction of taxes and subsidies
		Exchange rate and trade reforms
	Outputs, inputs are mostly internationally traded	Poverty and income distribution policies
	Government implements substantial production subsidies and trade intervention	Property rights reforms
2. Water depletion and degradation	Supply side is dominated by government or monopolies; bulk of resource use goes to large commercial enterprises and irrigation systems	Intersectoral pricing
		Reduction of subsidies and introduction of charges for resource degradation
	Resource is not internationally traded but sectoral use and productivity for main user groups substantially differ	
	Prices are highly regulated	
3. Energy use and air pollution	As with water, supply side dominated by government and monopolies	Exchange rate reforms
		Reduction of cross-subsidies
	Inputs (coal, oil) are generally traded; output broadly linked to all production activities	Privatization programs for generating and distribution activities
	Sectoral investment and pricing highly centralized	

5

Linkages Between the Environment
and Economywide Policies:
Recent World Bank Experience

THIS BOOK FOCUSES ON THE ENVIRONMENTAL IMPLICATIONS of
economywide policy reforms undertaken at the sectoral or
macroeconomic level. Economywide policies involve a variety
of economic instruments, ranging from pricing in key sectors
(for example, energy or water) and broad sectoral taxation or
subsidy programs (for example, agricultural production subsidies, industrial investment incentives); to macroeconomic
policies and strategies (exchange rate, interest rate, or wage
policies; trade liberalization, privatization, and so forth).
Economywide policies are packaged often within programs of
structural adjustment or sectoral reform, aimed at promoting
economic stability, efficiency and growth, and ultimately,
human welfare.

Our focus is on the linkages between economic policies and the environment; other key social objectives like popular participation, empowerment and the rights of indigenous peoples fall outside its scope. Nevertheless, the generic findings and approach presented here could be useful also in systemically identifying some of the underlying economic and environmental causes of a wider range of social, institutional and legal impacts, and therefore suggest directions for policy reform.

Although macroeconomic and sectoral policies are typically not directed explicitly towards influencing the quality of the natural environment, they may, nonetheless have major impacts upon it, either positive or negative. This chapter provides evidence from a number of studies to indicate that there are significant payoffs in attempting to better understand such impacts and to act upon them. Positive impacts of economywide reforms on the environment can be used to build constituencies for reform. Potential negative impacts need to be analyzed, monitored and mitigated. In some instances the *direction* of environmental impact stemming from economywide policy reform is fairly straightforward. The *extent* of the impact, however, invariably requires empirical analysis. In more complex cases, even the direction of the impact is ambiguous. In view of their location-specific nature, and the complexity of economic, physical, ecological, institutional and cultural variables involved, there is a clear need for more case study material to enhance our understanding of these relationships.

Building upon the experience of previous work, this chapter reviews some recent experience in the World Bank in this regard. Such experience has been obtained both from lending operations and sector studies as well as from specific, in-depth, research efforts. Although the case studies have been labeled as "research," they have been highly applied, and primarily carried out by staff with operational responsibilities within the Bank.

The studies themselves reflect a wide range of country situations and environmental problems. Thus pollution issues are addressed with reference to industrial pollution in Poland. Environmental aspects of energy use are addressed in the Sri Lanka case. A variety of natural resource related issues are covered in the other studies: deforestation and land degradation in Costa Rica, deforestation in the Philippines, degradation of agricultural lands due to overgrazing in Tunisia, fertility losses due to extension of cultivated areas in Ghana; water resource depletion in Morocco; and wildlife management in Zimbabwe. Some of the examples mentioned in this chapter are summarized more extensively in Chapter 6 of this book and Volume II.

The case studies utilize a variety of analytical methods to illustrate the different approaches available for identifying the environmental implications of economywide reforms. These methods range from those tracing the links between economic incentives and resource use through direct observation, to others relying on more complex economic modeling of policies and their environmental effects. In all the studies, however, the analytical approach uniformly requires identifying key environmental concerns and relating these to the agenda of priority sectoral and macroeconomic reforms under consideration. The analysis underscores the formidable difficulties of developing a general methodology to trace all possible environmental impacts of a package of adjustment reforms and until recently there has been relatively limited empirical work on this subject.[1] Nonetheless, the case studies offer evidence that careful case-specific empirical work may help identify better ways to deal with potentially serious impacts of specific economywide policies on high priority environmental problems. This chapter also indicates the considerable scope

---

[1]Exceptions include Reed (ed.) 1992; Mahar 1988; Cruz and Repetto 1992; Panayotou and Sussangkarn 1991.

for developing better analytical tools to trace environment-economic policy linkages.

General findings from the World Bank case studies and other experience are summarized below. One recurring theme is that the potential for achieving parallel gains in conventional economic, social and environmental goals is often present whenever economywide reforms attempt to improve macroeconomic stability, increase efficiency, and alleviate poverty. However, in important cases these potential gains cannot be realized unless complementary environmental and social measures are carried out. The results are elaborated below under the following headings:

- Efficiency Motivated Policies
- Other Policy, Market, or Institutional Imperfections
- Macroeconomic Stability
- Longer-Term Poverty and Income Distributional Effects

Efficiency Motivated Policies

The main feature of most policy reforms directed at various levels of economic decisionmaking are price changes which are designed to promote efficiency and reduce waste. The findings of this report reinforce the view that such programs which address price-related distortions ("getting prices right"), can contribute to both economic and environmental goals.

In many developing countries, misplaced efforts to promote specific regional or sectoral growth and general economic development have created complex webs of commodity, sectoral, and macroeconomic price distortions, resulting in economic inefficiency and stagnation. Often, these economic distortions also lead to unanticipated changes in production and input-use that promote resource overexploitation or pollution. Such economic distortions may arise from a macroeconomic policy (such as the overvaluation of the local currency) or from a sectoral policy with economywide implications (such as subsidized energy prices). In either case, economywide policies that are not designed for environmental purposes may have substantial effects on the level and conduct of environment-related activities, suggesting that correcting such price-related distortions will also result in environmental gains. Among the broadest remedies are those correcting the foreign exchange rate and taxes that distort trade. More sector-specific reforms seek to shift key relative prices—for example, setting efficient prices for energy or water (which have pervasive effects), and removing taxes or subsidies on particular commodities or factors of production.

Macroeconomic reforms

At the level of "macroeconomic" pricing policies, the **Zimbabwe** study illustrates how foreign exchange reforms associated with adjustment efforts can support a key environmental sector. Wildlife-based economic activities in Zimbabwe, including ecotourism, safaris, hunting, and specialized meat and hide production, constitute some of the fastest growing sectors. Wildlife-based tourism alone grew at the rate of 13 percent in 1991, comprising 5 percent of GDP. From the environmental perspective, wildlife-based activities (unlike cattle ranching which competes for limited land resources), are better suited to the country's semiarid climate and poor soils. Economically viable systems can be maintained with lower stocking rates and a reduced environmental burden, compared to cattle ranching and pastoral activities. Equally important is the indirect environmental benefit associated with wildlife management goals of conserving a natural habitat that appeals to visitors.

There is much interest in wildlife development in Zimbabwe, with emphasis placed on its potential role as a more sustainable land use system than cattle ranching or conventional agriculture, in semiarid zones. Wildlife enterprises currently account for 15 percent of land use on commercial and communal lands. Wildlife on which ecotourism is based competes with beef production—in terms of land use, rather than meat output. Despite its economic and environmental advantages, sectoral land policies have generally discouraged wildlife activities since these are still perceived as "underutilizing" land. Livestock marketing and pricing policies have also traditionally subsidized cattle ranching.

More importantly, for many years, the government's foreign exchange and trade policies severely penalized this sector. The Zimbabwean dollar was overvalued by 50 to 80 percent from 1981 to 1990. This meant that export-oriented sectors were implicitly taxed, among them wildlife and nature tourism concerns. Foreign exchange earnings were diverted to other sectors, depressing incomes and investment in wildlife. In 1990, the government introduced an adjustment package, including measures aimed at boosting the level of exports. The currency was devalued by 25 percent, and more liberal access to foreign exchange was allowed. These moves were beneficial on both economic and ecological fronts. Exports increased. At the same time, the profitability of the wildlife sector improved, leading to a significant increase of wildlife in commercial farmlands.

While the Zimbabwe study above illustrates how relatively straightforward and unambiguous links between macroeconomic reforms and specific environmental effects can be traced and measured, in other cases the effects of policy change are more indirect. Such indirect or system effects of economic policies on the environment have prompted some interest in the use of computable general equilibrium (CGE) models.

This approach has been used in the study of **Morocco**, which employed a CGE model linking agricultural water use to trade policies. Low water charges (coupled with ineffective collection of these charges), have artificially promoted production of water intensive crops such as sugar cane. Thus, rural irrigation water

accounts for 92 percent of the country's marketed water use. At the same time, irrigation charges cover less than 10 percent of the LRMC, while the corresponding figure for urban water tariffs is less than 50 percent. Given these policies, it is not surprising that a water deficit is projected for Morocco by the year 2020, notwithstanding the fact that by the same year, water sector investments would account for 60 percent of the government budget. The study, however, goes beyond the traditional sectoral remedy of proposing an increase in water tariffs. It links sectoral policy reforms with ongoing macroeconomic adjustment policies, involving the complete removal of nominal trade tariffs, and analyzes the overall effects of both sets of reforms.

In the CGE simulation, liberalization of trade alone leads to a marginal rise in real GDP. Household incomes and consumption post significant gains as import barriers are reduced, exports become more competitive, domestic purchasing power rises and resources are allocated more efficiently across the economy. The two major drawbacks, however, are that elimination of tariffs leads to budgetary deficits, and domestic water use increases substantially due to the expansionary effects of liberalization. In the second scenario, only water price reforms are considered. The results indicate (as expected) that, other things being equal, doubling water prices reduces water use significantly—by 34 percent in rural areas and by 29 percent for the economy as a whole. This static efficiency gain, however, is acquired at a price—real GDP falls by about 0.65 percent relative to what it would have been, and incomes and real consumption of both rural and urban households decline by approximately 1 percent.

In the final scenario, the trade liberalization continues to stimulate growth, but simultaneously reforming water prices induces substantial reductions in agricultural (and economywide) water use, unlike in the scenario involving price reform alone. To summarize, the macroeconomic policy reform (trade liberalization) alone resulted in more efficient allocation of resources and expansion of exports, but also led to environmental stress through increased water use. When complementary water price increases were simultaneously undertaken with trade liberalization, the beneficial expansionary economic effects of the latter were largely retained, but now with substantial reductions in water use as well (due to the higher water prices).

Sectoral reforms

More specific or restricted policies affecting major sectors, such as industry and agriculture, or key resources, like energy, are also addressed in programs of economywide policy reforms. For example, the potential gains from price reform in the energy sector may be enormous. In fact, all recent energy projects supported by the World Bank have involved careful assessment of the adequacy of institutional arrangements and price efficiency. In each case efforts were made to promote rational pricing policies, improve institutional effectiveness, and achieve greater transparency and accountability in the provision of energy.

Energy sector reforms can contribute to both economic and environmental goals. In **Sri Lanka**, for example, as in most developing countries, electricity prices have been well below the incremental cost of future supplies. Many studies show that eliminating power subsidies by raising tariffs closer to the LRMC of power generation, will encourage more efficient use of electricity.[2] In projecting future electricity requirements in Sri Lanka, the study found that the economic benefits of setting electricity prices to reflect LRMC is supplemented by an unambiguously favorable impact on the environment. In addition, pricing reforms were found to have better economic and environmental impacts than purely technical approaches to demand-side manage-

ment, such as promoting the use of energy-saving fluorescent lights. Of course, a combination of both pricing and technical measures provided the best results.

This emphasis is reflected in two recent World Bank policy papers for the energy sector.[3] As noted earlier, one of these reports estimates that developing countries spend more than US$250 billion annually on subsidizing energy.[4] The countries of the former U.S.S.R. and Eastern Europe account for the bulk of this amount (US$180 billion), and it is estimated that more than half of their air pollution is attributable to such price distortions. Removing all energy subsidies would produce large gains in efficiency and in fiscal balances, and would sharply reduce local pollution and cut carbon emissions by as much as 20 percent in some countries, and by about 7 percent worldwide.

Similarly, electricity prices in developing countries are, on average, barely more than one-third of supply costs. As a result, consumers use about 20 percent more electricity than they would if they paid the true costs of supply. Moreover, recent evidence shows that far from correcting this distortion, many governments have been slow to adjust electricity tariffs to reflect higher costs from inflation, fuel, and interest charges. A review of electricity tariffs in 60 developing countries has shown that average tariffs declined over the period 1979–88 from US$0.052–US$0.038 per kWh (1986 U.S. dollars).[5] This is particularly troubling as energy demands are expected to grow, and will probably double in the next 15 years. Achieving commercial pricing policies is, therefore, central to achieving energy efficiency and economic sustainability. Consequently of the 24 energy and power sector loans approved by the World

---

[2]Munasinghe 1990.

[3]World Bank 1993b, World Bank 1993k.

[4]World Bank 1993b.

[5]World Bank 1993k.

Bank in fiscal year 1993, 16 contained specific requirements to adjust energy prices.

The negative environmental effects of industrial protection policies also suggest the win-win potential of industrial policy reforms. This is illustrated in the experience of **Mexico** from 1970 to the late 1980s. Between 1970 to 1989, industrial pollution intensity (per unit of value added) in Mexico increased by 25 percent, induced by government investments and subsidies in the petrochemical and fertilizer industries. The energy intensity of industry also increased by 5.7 percent in the same period. Aside from the beneficial environmental aspects of removing such subsidies, there will also be direct fiscal implications. Energy subsidies are generally costly, and must be financed from government budgets that are often in deficit. In Mexico, broad subsidies for fuels and electricity absorbed US$8–US$13 billion, or 4–7 percent of GDP, from 1980 to 1985. (See Box 5–1.)

Box 5–1: Fiscal Policy and Air Pollution in Mexico

A recent study addressed the environmental consequences of industrial growth in Mexico, in terms of air pollution and changes in energy intensity of industrial output. The impact of industrial development on the environment has been substantial. Industrial production increased by a factor of 10 between 1950 and 1989. With respect to pollution, the study results suggested that the environment did not only deteriorate as a result of the growth of manufacturing output but also due to a considerable shift towards the more polluting subsectors leading to an increase in the pollution intensity, that is the amount of emissions per unit of manufacturing output.

Between 1950 and 1970 the pollution intensity of the manufacturing industry (calculated with fixed emission coefficients) increased by 50 percent. The growing participation of the production of highly polluting intermediates in total manufacturing output was the main cause of this increase. The study also showed that industrial pollution intensity increased by another 25 percent from 1970 to 1989, particularly in the second half of this period. This increase is almost completely explained by the growth of public sector investments from 1978 to 1982 in the petrochemical and fertilizer industries. The pollution intensity figures used in the study were derived from U.S. emissions data for 1987 using fixed pollution coefficients by subsector. Thus, changes in the estimates of total industrial pollution intensity are completely produced by structural shifts in the composition of manufacturing output. Neither the possibility of technology choice nor the influence of economic policies, for example trade policies, on this choice were taken into account in the estimates.

To complement this analysis, the energy intensity of Mexican industry in relation to energy pricing policies between 1970 and 1990 was examined. It was found that energy pricing policies led to annual implicit subsidies for energy products (that is, petroleum fuels, gas, and electricity) of between US$8 billion and US$13 billion, or 4 to 7 percent of GDP, from 1980 to 1985. Associated with this, the energy intensity of Mexican industry increased by 5.7 percent from 1970 to 1990 while industrial energy intensity in OECD countries decreased by 35.3 percent over the same period.

An increase in petroleum fuel and electricity intensity appears to be almost exclusively attributable to technological and other changes within subsectors, and not to structural shifts in production towards more energy intensive sectors. To some extent, the failure of Mexican industry to follow the trends towards energy saving adopted by the OECD countries after the oil price shocks of 1973 and 1979 could be attributed to the government policy of keeping energy prices far below international levels in the late 1970s and early 1980s. The more recent reduction of implicit subsidies to energy is expected to induce a lower increase of energy demand during a period of renewed economic growth.

The study found no evidence to support the view that foreign trade policies were to blame for the growth in industrial pollution. Pollution has resulted mainly from structural changes, such as the increasing importance of intermediates and public investment in the heavily polluting petro- and agro-chemical industries, and also from the low pricing policies for publicly provided petroleum fuels and electricity. By contrast, foreign trade policies have been strongly biased in favor of the less polluting consumer good industries.

Box 5-1. continued.

In addition to environmental aspects of industrialization for the whole country, studies have also addressed the specific problem of air pollution in Mexico City. Exacerbated by low fuel prices, air quality in Mexico City has steadily declined in recent years. Efficient air quality management requires, *inter alia*, that pollution reductions be obtained from the least costly source. Taxing pollution directly would conform with this prescription, since it would provide incentives to firms and individuals to pursue emissions reductions in the least costly manner. However, because Mexico City's sources of pollution are many and varied (buses, taxis, and private vehicles, all of varying ages), each vehicle's emissions cannot be monitored continuously, so it is not feasible to tax emissions directly.

This suggests the need to develop indirect instruments, which target proxies for emissions (for example, indicators of how clean the car is and how much it is used). These indicators could be influenced by regulations such as emissions standards, and market-based tools such as fuel taxes. The latter are particularly relevant where, as has traditionally been the case in Mexico, fuel prices are well below their opportunity costs. In fact, the general conclusion stemming from this study is that the appropriate policy for combating vehicular air pollution consists of two elements, namely, policies aimed at making vehicles and fuels cleaner, and policies aimed at reducing demand for trips. To reduce emissions by modifying fuels and vehicles, some measures will be best implemented by regulation, others by market-based instruments. But when it comes to reducing demand, taxation is immensely more effective than regulations, which often limit choices unnecessarily. The study in fact concludes that by combining such an environmental tax instrument with regulatory approaches, targeted emissions reductions can be obtained with savings of at least 10 percent of the cost of "regulation-only" approaches.

The inadequacy of reliance upon regulatory methods was exemplified by Mexico City's one day-a-week driving ban, a measure that could have been effective on a temporary basis, but which proved ineffective when applied permanently. Gasoline taxes, in contrast—now being forcefully applied in Mexico—manage demand by screening out only the least essential trips. They also have the advantage of raising public revenues, as well as reducing road congestion and accidents.

Source: Ten Kate 1993; Eskeland 1992, 1993.

Energy subsidies are not the only form of policy-induced inefficiency. Many natural resources are subsidized, leading to distorted investment decisions and removing competitive incentives to use them efficiently. Unfortunately, subsidies tend to create powerful beneficiaries who come to regard their subsidy as a right, creating challenging political and institutional obstacles to full cost pricing. A recent Bank Operations Evaluation Department (OED) review of experience in urban water supply and sanitation projects between 1967 and 1989, for example, found that borrowers often fail to comply with covenants, especially those on pricing and financial performance. Another OED review of completed irrigation projects, found that cost recovery was unsatisfactory in 73 percent of the 107 projects surveyed. The Bank has taken steps to strengthen cost recovery mechanisms because benefits from removing subsidies can be substantial, economically, environmentally and socially—especially when such subsidies benefit large-scale users of a resource and the

funds could be used to alleviate poverty more directly.

Experience in the water and sanitation sector illustrates the limitations of direct government provision and indiscriminate subsidization of household services. Despite progress in developing affordable engineering solutions, the delivery and maintenance of services have often been disappointing. Subsidies are often captured by wealthier customers, and in most situations resources are inadequate to maintain a high quality of service or to extend facilities to low income areas. Subsidies may be justified in specific situations (rural water supplies in low income areas and sewage treatment in urban areas), but these are most effective when targeted and explicit. Thus, water and sanitation projects approved by the World Bank are increasingly emphasizing cost recovery.

The negative effects of underpricing resources can also be seen in the agricultural sector. In **Tunisia**, the government's concern with ensuring sufficient supply and affordability of livestock products has resulted in a web of pricing and subsidy interventions. A variety of subsidies has promoted livestock production intensification in certain parts of Tunisia, while in other regions they have encouraged herd maintenance at levels beyond rangelands' carrying capacity. Particularly during dry years, subsidized feed imports have substituted for natural pasture, and have averted herd contraction. This failure of herds to respond to diminished feed availability in natural pastures, however, has contributed to significant rangeland degradation primarily in the central and southern regions of the country. This has direct effects on livestock production, and long-term, indirect implications for the entire agriculture sector.

In the past few years, several further examples of the adverse environmental effects of these types of economywide policies have been examined. Bank studies on **Brazil** have demonstrated the role of sectoral policies subsidizing frontier land clearing and use that have exacerbated deforestation in the Amazon.[6]

Other Policy, Market, or Institutional Imperfections

While liberalizing policies typically help both the economy and the environment, unaddressed policy, market and institutional failures may undermine the beneficial environmental effects of economywide reforms. The reform process is typically handled in stages, with the initial adjustment package aimed at the most important macroeconomic issues. Some distortions that policymakers intend to address later in the adjustment process, or

other constraints that have passed unnoticed in the initial screening, often cause environmental harm. Paralleling the way in which the social consequences of adjustment should be handled, such potential adverse environmental consequences due to remaining inefficiencies or inequities in the economic system may therefore require additional measures to be introduced, to complement the original economywide policies.[7]

Policy distortions that remain need to be addressed to ensure environmental gains

Reforms in energy prices will help the environment, but remaining policy distortions elsewhere may reduce the beneficial effect. This is exemplified in the Poland case study, where energy intensity and excessive pollution have been caused by not only the undervaluation of coal in the centralized price system but also the entire system of state ownership that suppressed market signals and incentives. Previous research had already shown how economywide adjustments, including increases in energy prices, contributed to improvements in energy use and pollution in Poland.[8] The current study indicates, however, that energy intensity and excessive pollution in Poland is due not only to the undervaluation of coal in the centralized price system but more importantly, to the entire system of state ownership that encourages output maximization rather than cost minimization. This means that price responsiveness is blunted, since financial losses are simply absorbed by the public budget, or passed on to consumers in the form of higher output prices.

The Poland study points out the special challenges that the Former Soviet Union and other countries of Central and Eastern Europe face as they attempt to restructure their economies and make a rapid transition to the market system. All of these economies are more

---

[6]Mahar 1988 and Binswanger 1989 have analyzed the role of subsidies to agricultural expansion as the key factor leading to deforestation. Schneider 1993 focuses on institutional barriers at the economic frontier that prevent the emergence of land tenure services, such as titling and property rights enforcement, and thus undermines the potential for sustainable land use.

---

[7]Munasinghe, Cruz, and Warford 1993.

[8]Hughes 1992.

material intensive than market economies, as soft budget constraints and centralized plans lead to maximization of output and resource use, rather than cost minimization. The high energy intensity endemic to all socialist economies is manifested in Poland's case through excessive reliance on coal. The study also indicates that, especially in the case of economies in rapid transition, regulations, institutions, and so forth, should not be allowed to lag too far behind economic restructuring.

In 1990, Poland initiated an economic transformation program that led to the privatization of many enterprises. The program was adversely affected by recession and the collapse of trading arrangements linked to the Council of Mutual Economic Assistance (CMEA). Furthermore, the process of privatization proved to be more complex and lengthy than initially expected. The government has therefore introduced an enterprise and bank restructuring program to assist in the restructuring of state-owned enterprises (SOEs) and in reducing their debt-servicing constraints.

Despite these changes, SOEs will continue to be major players in the Polish economy, at least in the short term. Of particular relevance is the decision by the government to retain ownership in the energy, mining, steel and defense sectors in the medium term, and to decide on privatization on a case-by-case basis over the next three years. Thus, energy sector restructuring efforts have focused on creating the institutional and legal framework to facilitate competition and greater private sector participation in the future. Coupled with aggressive energy pricing reforms, this strategy appears to be making some headway. For example, a recent survey of large state-owned manufacturing concerns found that even without privatization, SOEs are already adjusting to the transformation program. In particular, the survey found that all firms reduced their consumption of materials and energy per unit of sales.

The same generic set of issues is encountered in **China**, with specific reference to sustainable agriculture. Dramatic reforms have included reductions in subsidies for chemical fertilizers and pesticides, increases in energy prices, lifting of quotas for key agricultural products, and reduced intervention in product markets. A new study focused on farm-level decisionmaking in Dafeng County, Jiangsu Province, where rapid industrialization is occurring and the opportunity cost of labor has increased considerably in recent years. (See Box 5–2.) Application of crop and animal residues as fertilizer (a labor-intensive activity) has been discouraged by current trends in labor costs, thereby stimulating excessive demand for chemical fertilizer which may be less environmentally desirable. Increases in commercial energy prices may also result in burning of biomass. Another potential problem arises from the fact that one major agricultural input, namely land, is still subject to command and control and, in some communities, arbitrariness in its allocation. In such circumstances, the uncertainty about land allocation tends to encourage short-run profit maximization and exploitation of land at the expense of sustainability in agricultural prouction. Land access issues are also relevant in the institutional reforms discussed below.

Market failures may lead to environmentally costly patterns of growth

Aside from existing policy distortions, the absence of price signals for environmental services can undermine the contribution of efficiency- and growth-promoting reforms. However, recent studies on high-growth economies indicate that addressing environmental concerns early in the transition to growth may allow countries to limit the adverse environmental impacts of expanded economic activity. For example, a recent study on mitigating pollution and congestion impacts in the high-growth economy of Thailand concludes that environmental effects are not solely determined by the scale of economic

Box 5–2: Economic Transition and Sustainable Agriculture in China

Chinese significant transformations are taking place in agriculture in the context of rapid evolution in the economy. Dramatic, economywide changes have taken place in the relative prices of relevant farm inputs, including reduction in subsidies for chemical fertilizers and pesticides, and increases in the price of energy, and the opportunity cost of labor. Changes in other government policies also affect environmental behavior, via their influence on prices. Among these are lifting of quotas for key agricultural products and substantial reduction in intervention in product markets. Other important changes relate to policy and practice regarding government support for eco-farming and security of land tenure.

Using farm-level data from communities in Dafeng County, Jiangsu Province, an ongoing assessment of sustainable agriculture illustrates the vast range of variables that determine environmental behavior. The area has been experiencing rapid industrial development, and the opportunity cost of labor has increased rapidly in recent years. This trend in labor cost discourages the application of crop and animal residues to the land—a labor-intensive activity. Increases in commercial energy prices may also result in the diversion of biomass for fuel, thereby stimulating demand for chemical fertilizer. Alternatively, where cotton is produced (perhaps to meet a government quota), cotton waste, which has little environmental value, may be burned instead. In assessing the environmental policy implications of changes in the prices of key inputs, the study makes it clear that "second best" problems abound. For example, one major agricultural input, namely land, is still subject to command and control and, in some communities, arbitrariness in its allocation. In such circumstances, the uncertainty about land tenure generated by this system has encouraged short-run profit maximization and exploitation of land at the expense of sustainability in agricultural production.

Surveys of farmers' reaction to changes in strategic prices and policy variables suggest ways in which they might react in the future under various scenarios of price and other policy reform. Based on the assumption that farmers are profit maximizers, farm models are being designed to simulate reaction to various scenarios of future changes in the prices of inputs and outputs, for example, by crop switching, reducing scale of operations, changing mix of inputs, or going out of business. The environmental implications of these reactions, and therefore the need for possible remedial action, will then be assessed.

Policies are rapidly evolving, but the relevance of this study, location-specific though it is, is in illustrating the leverage exerted by macro-level and sectoral policies on farmers' behavior and therefore, by definition, upon the environment. It also suggests that while market liberalization is a necessary condition to encourage farmers to operate efficiently and thereby to ensure that neither producers nor consumers use resources wastefully, it is far from a sufficient condition for sound environmental management. Market reforms need to be accompanied by various forms of public intervention. This may take the form of education and training to bring farmers up to date with latest techniques. However, where modern techniques and the changes in the relative prices of key agricultural inputs yield unsatisfactory environmental by-products, the study illustrates the kind of situation in which government should be prepared to step in and compensate for market failure. Above all it demonstrates that policy reform in the environmental area, while urgent, has to parallel overall trends in market liberalization in the Chinese economy.

Source: Hu and Warford 1994.

activity—the "structure of the economy, the efficiency of input use (especially in energy and industry) and the types of production technologies in use all matter in determining the environmental impacts" of economic growth.[9]

The specific role of market failure in influencing the environmental implications of economic reforms is illustrated in the case of liberalization policies and industrial promo-

tion in **Indonesia**. In this case, adjustment reforms which are successful in the traditional sense of stimulating industrial growth may have adverse pollution consequences because of market failure—no price signals prevent excessive buildup of pollution. Accelerated industrial growth, while clearly desirable for poverty reduction, could therefore bring with it increased pollution. (See Box 5–3.)

The Indonesia case shows how reforms can mitigate some of the pollution problems associated with growth. In terms of emissions

---

[9]World Bank 1994c.

per unit of output, or pollution intensity, the study found that processing industries (for example, food products, pulp, and paper) tend to be dirtier than assembly (for example, garments and furniture) industries. Liberalization in the 1980s promoted a surge in assembly industries, thereby reversing the 1970s pattern of more rapid growth in "dirty" processing sectors. Projections indicate that the share of basic processing industries in total industrial output will fall from 72 percent in 1993 to about 60 percent by 2020.

In addition, industry expanded rapidly outside densely populated Java, reducing the health impact of industrial concentration. However, industrial output growth has been so rapid that general pollution levels have nevertheless increased. Thus, while decreases in pollution intensity and industrial decentralization have helped to limit pollution, formal regulations will need to be strengthened also, to avoid health and environmental damage in the future.

Pervasive institutional constraints may undermine potentially beneficial environmental impacts of policy reforms

The nature of macroeconomic effects on the environment is also contingent upon prevailing regulations or institutions governing resource use. The current case studies indicate that institutional constraints are a pervasive problem, and that they take many forms. For example, the eventual impact of economywide reforms (such as those affecting international and domestic terms of trade) on the incentives facing farm households will be influenced by intervening institutional factors (which are themselves determined by cultural, economic, and political factors)—especially those affecting access and use rights over agricultural resources such as land and water.

The role of institutional constraints in macroeconomic reform programs is examined in the **Ghana** case study. In this example, trade liberalization, by reducing the taxation of agricultural exports leads to increased production incentives, while efforts to reduce the government wage bill tend to increase the pool of unemployed. Thus, the adjustment process helps to stimulate production of export crops, and combines with rapid population growth and lack of employment opportunities outside the rural sector to create increasing pressure on land resources, encroachment onto marginal lands, and soil erosion. This effect on resource use is influenced by the allocation of property rights. Whether in relation to the security of land tenure of peasant farmers, or to the right to extract timber by logging companies, uncertainty normally results in environmental degradation. In Ghana, as in many regions of Africa, agricultural lands are governed by traditional land use institutions, and farms are communally owned by the village or tribe. These common property regimes may have been sufficient in allowing sustainable use of agricultural lands when populations were much smaller, and sufficient fallow periods could allow land to regain its fertility. However, such traditional arrangements would be overwhelmed ultimately by economywide forces, resulting in reduced fallowing, loss of soil fertility and environmental decline. The foregoing suggests that better clarification of property rights may help to resist externally induced pressures.

In the **China** case study discussed earlier, economywide pricing reforms in output markets have not been accompanied by similar reforms on the input side. Land resources are, of course, among the major agricultural inputs, and uncertainty may persist about future rights to farm individual plots of land in many localities, even as agricultural markets in general are being liberalized. This could worsen the incentives for short-term overexploitation of land resources, leading to degradation. (See Box 5–2.)

Relevant laws and regulations governing resource access should be reviewed when economywide reforms are planned, especially when there is evidence that key resource sectors such as land, forests, minerals, or

Box 5–3. Industrial Growth and Pollution in Indonesia

The trade liberalization experience in Indonesia shows that while economic policy reforms can promote less pollution intensive industrialization, the rapid expansion of the scale of industrial activity points to the urgent need for regulation as a complement to economic policy reforms. A recent study decomposed industrial pollution in Indonesia by breaking it down into three dimensions: (a) the pollution intensity of output, (b) its location relative to human populations and fragile ecosystems, and (c) the increase in absolute levels of pollutants due to the expansion of output. Using industrial data from 1975 to 1989, the likely impact of continuing reforms on the scale and structure of pollution was then projected to the year 2020.

Secondly, the sectoral characteristics of pollution-intensive activities were examined, by classifying them according to indicators of air, water, and toxic pollution per unit of output. Materials processing industries (for example, food products, tobacco, pulp and paper, basic industrial chemicals, petroleum refineries, iron and steel) were generally found to score higher on these indicators than assembly type industries (for example, garments, furniture and fixtures, printing and publishing, metal products, office and computing machinery, transport equipment). For example, the ratio of air pollution intensities in assembly to processing industries ranged from 2.4 to 6.1.

Finally, the impact of liberalization on all three dimensions of pollution and on the pollution characteristics of different industrial sectors were assessed. The analysis showed that liberalization in the 1980s promoted a surge in relatively clean assembly processes, reversing the 1970s pattern of more rapid growth in "dirty" materials-processing sectors. Projections indicate that the share of basic processing industries in total industrial output will fall from 72 percent in 1993 to about 60 percent by 2020.

In addition to changes in composition of output, within Indonesia liberalization efforts were also associated with differentially rapid growth of "dirty" sectors outside the densely populated island of Java, thereby reducing the health and productivity impact of pollution on population centers. On Java, assembly industries have grown faster than processing activities, and will probably be larger than the latter by the year 2020. However, processing industries outside Java will continue to account for about 80 percent of industrial output.

While reforms contributed to mitigating the impact of pollution from these two sources, industrial growth has been so rapid that the scale effect dominates current patterns and future trends in industrial pollution. Industry has responded very strongly to liberalization; manufacturing output has doubled in volume every six to seven years during the 1970s and 1980s, so that in 1990 manufacturing value added was about eight times its 1970 level in real terms. This accelerated growth, while clearly desirable for poverty reduction, has nevertheless undermined the positive impacts of liberalization on reduced pollution intensity and the relocation of "dirty" industries. Thus, Indonesian industry in the aftermath of liberalization has a much-improved sectoral and locational profile from an environmental perspective. However, accelerated growth has pushed pollution to new heights almost everywhere. Efforts to augment the reform program with institutional support and regulation will clearly be required if Indonesia is to avoid severe pollution problems in the future.

Source: Wheeler and Martin 1993.

marine resources will be affected. A useful example of how such programs could incorporate legal reforms for environmental purposes is the recent adjustment operation undertaken in **Peru**. In this example, it was determined that economywide reforms to promote economic recovery could potentially increase harvesting pressures on Peru's overexploited fisheries. Thus, the complementary new fishing regulations to protect various fishing grounds were incorporated directly into the adjustment program.[10]

Another common institutional problem relates not to the rules and regulations themselves, but rather to the government's capacity to establish and enforce such rules. Regulating large numbers of potentially environmentally degrading activities is especially difficult, even for industrial country governments.

Substantial reductions in institutional and monitoring needs may be achieved with the use of indirect measures or modified pricing-regulation approaches. This is illustrated, for example, by the Mexico City air pollution study which shows that while, in principle, pollution taxes are the most accurate means of

---

[10]World Bank 1993g.

achieving reductions in pollutants, in practice, administrative feasibility demands that less refined instruments such as taxes on consumption of fuels may have to be used. While recourse to blunt instruments will help, the magnitude of the institutional capacity-building challenge nevertheless remains clear. Building the relevant institutional capacity in developing countries therefore should be underscored, and appropriate resources should be made available early in the adjustment process to assist country governments in this task.

Macroeconomic Stability

Sustainable resource management requires economic stability

One broad objective of structural adjustment lending is to help restore stability in countries beset by economic crises. A recent example involves the Sub-Saharan countries, where a Bank study concludes: "No economy can function well for long if it has rampant inflation, an overvalued exchange rate, excessive taxation of the agricultural sector, scarce supplies of needed inputs, regulations on prices and production, deficient public services, and limited financial services."[11] The causes of macroeconomic instability often arise from imbalances created by long-standing, internal policy failures and aggravated by adverse external conditions. For example, a history of policies which have allowed increased domestic spending without parallel growth in production eventually leads to inflation or current accounts deficits or both. When unfavorable external credit or trade conditions arise, the result is macroeconomic instability. Under these conditions, both government budget deficits and international trade balances progressively deteriorate. When an external shock occurs (such as an increase in the prices of imported energy or a decline in

the prices of the country's main exports), the result is macroeconomic instability of crisis proportions.

The relationship between environmental issues and policy reforms is fairly straightforward at this general level. Macroeconomic instability is not only disastrous for the economy, but also frequently detrimental to the environment. For example, high interest rates associated with economic crises can severely undermine the value of sustainable production, as resource outputs in the future lose most of their expected value. Thus, to the extent that adjustment policies can help restore macroeconomic stability, their impact will be unambiguously beneficial for long-term natural resource management and environmental concerns. This link is illustrated in the **Costa Rica** case study, which used a macroeconomic model incorporating timber harvesting activities, to examine the deforestation implications of various macroeconomic factors. Simulation results demonstrate that lower interest rates associated with a stable economy allow the logging sector to correctly anticipate benefits from future returns to forestry, thereby leading to a decline in current logging activities.[12]

Other studies have indicated that low and stable discount rates favor the choice of sustainable farming rather than short-term cultivation practices.[13] This is important since "mining" of agricultural land resources is often the prevailing form of resource use in many tropical areas. Frontier farmers have to choose between a sustainable production system with stable but low yields and

---

[12]The effect of inadequate tenurial security over the resource (and future benefits from it) parallel the results for high discount rates. This corresponds to the well-known result in renewable resource exploitation models that the effects on economic behavior of open-access resource conditions are formally equivalent to those of having secure property rights with infinitely high discount rates.

---

[11]World Bank 1994a, p. 37.

[13]Southgate and Pearce 1988.

unsustainable practices which initially have high yields. Using farm models and data from **Brazil**,[14] a recent Bank study found that if interest rates are very high, farmers would tend to choose less sustainable methods. For example, at interest rates of 40 percent (the prevailing real interest rates at the time of the study),farmers would pursue unsustainable agricultural practices that yielded high initial returns but led to subsequent annual declines in productivity of 10 percent. This explains why agricultural land "mining" is so prevalent in the Amazon—since most sustainable farming technologies available to Brazilian farmers cannot provide such high incomes. The critical macroeconomic implication of this result is that attempts to resolve the land degradation problem solely by focusing on providing better agricultural technologies would probably be ineffective. To arrest land degradation, macroeconomic reforms which reduce the real interest rate would be needed.

Longer-Term Poverty and Income Distributional Effects

In addition to the short-term concerns discussed earlier, the crucial long-term links between poverty and environmental degradation in developing countries are increasingly being recognized (Refer to Box 4–4, on Poverty and the Environment.) Growing evidence of the relationship between reducing poverty and addressing environmental goals points to the need to undertake poverty and population programs as part of environmental efforts. The need to break the cycle of poverty, population growth, and environmental degradation has also been identified in a recent report of the International Development Association as a key challenge for sustainable development.[15]

An important result of examining the general equilibrium effects of macroeconomic

policy is that indirect resource allocation effects are important and may dominate the more direct effects of some price or income policy changes. In the **Costa Rica** study, the economic and environmental implications of wage restraints in structural adjustment are examined with the use of a CGE model which highlights the economic activities and factors affecting deforestation in Costa Rica. The model differs from standard approaches in two important respects. First, it can simulate the effect of introducing property rights on forest resources, thus allowing the private valuation of future forestry returns to contribute to sustainable management. Second, it also includes markets for logs and cleared land—loggers deforest to sell timber to the forest industry and squatters clear land for agricultural production and for sale to the agriculture sector (as the latter expands and requires more land).

The importance of indirect effects in Costa Rica is demonstrated in the analysis of economywide policy changes, such as an increase in the wage rate. Because the role of intersectoral resource flows is incorporated in the CGE model, the effects of changes in wages are different from partial equilibrium results. If the wage of unskilled labor were increased due to, say, minimum wage legislation, the model predicts that deforestation could worsen rather than decline. Although logging declines due to increased direct costs, this is more than made up by the indirect effect of intersectoral flows since the industrial sector (where minimum wage legislation is more binding) is much more adversely affected by the higher labor costs. Labor and capital thus tend to flow from industry to agriculture, leading to greater conversion of forest land for farming.

This simulation exercise suggests the need for caution in attempting to "legislate" income improvements by increasing minimum wages. Introducing higher wages initially improves labor incomes but a resulting contraction of industrial and agricultural employment leads

---

[14]Schneider 1993.

[15]International Development Association 1992.

not only to more unemployment but to environmental degradation as well. The increase in unemployment results in greater pressures for expanding shifting cultivation in forest lands.

Beyond pricing and intersectoral environmental linkages that can be identified in general equilibrium approaches, another set of studies has looked at the environmental implications of rural poverty and unemployment within the broader context of the social and demographic problems of inequitable land access and rapid population growth.[16] Import substitution, industrial protection, and regressive taxation are some economywide policies that have historically been associated with lagging employment generation, income inequality, and poverty. Unequal distribution of resources and inappropriate tenure are institutional factors that also contribute to the problem. In the context of inequitable assignment of endowments and rapid population growth, the resulting unemployment and income inequality force the poor to depend increasingly on marginal resources for their livelihood. The result is pressure on fragile environments. This effect can be analyzed in conjunction with the assessment of large migration episodes. These may occur as part of direct resettlement programs or may be induced by inappropriate policies, such as land colonization programs.

With regard to sustainable agriculture concerns, the World Bank study of the *Population, Environment and Agriculture Nexus in Sub-Saharan Africa* explicitly links the related problems of rapid population growth, agricultural stagnation and land degradation in Africa.[17] The study found that shifting cultivation and grazing in the context of limited capital and technical change cannot cope with rapid population growth. At the same time, the traditional technological solution of relying on high yielding crop varieties is not available. Thus, the study identified the need for a mix of responses in terms of reforms to remove subsidies for inappropriate land uses, improve land use planning, recognize property rights, provide better education, and construct appropriate rural infrastructure to promote production incentives.

Among the current Bank research, the **Philippines** case study evaluates the policy determinants of long-term changes in rural poverty and unemployment that have motivated increasing lowland to upland migration. This process has led to the conversion of forest lands to unsustainable agriculture and has been identified as a key mechanism contributing to the deforestation problem. The inability of the government to manage forest resources is an important direct cause of deforestation, but there is increasing recognition that economic policies, both sectoral and economywide, also significantly contribute to the problem. For example, the study links lowland poverty to agricultural taxation, price controls, and marketing restrictions, and uses an econometric model to demonstrate that the poverty contributes significantly to migration pressures on forest lands.

Trade and exchange rate policies have also played important roles in the Philippines and have been dominated by an urban consumer and industrial sector bias. The agricultural sector was implicitly taxed by an average of about 20 percent for most of the 1970s and early 1980s. Because the industrial sector did not provide an alternative source of growth, poverty generally has worsened and rural incomes in particular have suffered. The study results indicate that the main mechanism by which these economic problems affect the environment is through migration and the conversion of forest lands to unsustainable agriculture. Population pressure already evident in the 1970s worsened during the 1980s. The net upland migration rate grew from 3.4 to 9.4 percent between 1970 to 1975 and 1978 to 1980, and increased substantially to 14.5

---

[16]Feder et al. 1988; Cruz and Gibbs 1990; Lele and Stone 1989.

[17]Cleaver and Schreiber 1991.

percent between 1980 and 1985. Consequently, upland cropped area grew at annual
rates exceeding 7 percent from 1971 to 1987.
These results suggest that while forestry

specific conservation programs are needed,
economywide policy reforms could be as
important in arresting the process of deforestation.

6

Case Study Summaries

HIGHLIGHTS OF THE STUDIES forming the World Bank
research program on the linkages between economywide
policies and the environment are presented below. These
studies have been carefully selected to reflect a wide range
of country situations, and of environmental problems. The
very diversity of the cases considered is intended to demonstrate the generality of the overall theme—which is the
actual or potentially major impact that economic policies
have on the environment.

The cases include countries in Latin America (Costa Rica); Sub-Saharan Africa (Zimbabwe and Ghana); North Africa (Tunisia, Morocco); Asia (Philippines and Sri Lanka); and Eastern Europe (Poland). Various results from these case studies have been included in this book, as examples pertinent to specific policy issues. (For continuity of presentation, some of the points mentioned in the main text are repeated in the country summaries.) For the reader wishing to obtain further information, these studies are contained in Volume II.

Costa Rica[1]

While the other studies described in this chapter (except the Morocco study) generally adopt a partial equilibrium approach in addressing the environmental consequences of economic policy, it is clear that general equilibrium effects are important. Indeed, failure to protect the environment may have serious feedbacks and may constrain economic development. To capture this whole economy perspective a study of the linkages between economic policies and the environment in Costa Rica uses a computable general equilibrium (CGE) model. The model pays special attention to deforestation, which is proceeding at a rapid pace in Costa Rica. Together with soil erosion, it has been identified as the main environmental problem of the country.

Even conservative estimates of remaining forest cover forecast that if current deforestation rates continue, the commercial forests of Costa Rica will be exhausted within the next five years. To evaluate how sectoral and economywide policies can help control deforestation, the study constructed a CGE model that highlights the economic activities and factors affecting deforestation in Costa Rica. The model differs from standard

approaches in two important respects. First, it can simulate the effect of introducing property rights on forest resources, thus allowing the private valuation of future forestry returns to contribute to sustainable management. Second, it also includes markets for logs and cleared land: loggers deforest to sell timber to the forest industry and squatters clear land for agricultural production and for sale to the agriculture sector as the latter expands and requires more land.

The model retains features that are fairly standard in most CGE models. The tradable sectors—forestry, agriculture, and industry—are price takers in the world market, while infrastructure and services produce nontraded output. To focus on the natural resource sectors, the domestically mobile factors include, aside from capital and labor, cleared land and logs. The supplies of both labor and capital are exogenous. The demand for these factors arises from the producing sectors (agriculture, industry, and so forth) and from the deforestation activity of loggers and squatters. The supply of "cleared" land is initially based on Costa Rica's total land area that has been deforested. However, additional cleared land is made available from increased deforestation. This rate of land clearing depends on the definition of property rights as well as on taxes (or subsidies) that affect the forest and agricultural sectors. In addition, the expansion of squatting activities augments the cleared land factor. Agricultural production provides the demand for cleared land.

The results of the CGE simulations support the conventional view that establishing property rights tends to decrease deforestation. The reason is that such rights allow the logging sector to capture the future benefits of reducing excessive logging damage on residual stands. Initially, this loss is presumed to be 28 percent of the value of the residual stand. Using an interest rate of 10 percent, the simulation indicates that deforestation is dramatically reduced to 5 percent

---

[1]Researchers: Annika Persson and Mohan Munasinghe.

of the base level as both the logging and squatters sectors internalize the losses associated with deforestation. Significant reductions in deforestation occur even when the estimate of logging damage is substantially reduced. The CGE results on the deforestation effects of discount rate changes also parallel the predictions of partial equilibrium models: higher interest rates promote deforestation while lower interest rates contribute to conservation.

Beyond augmenting the analysis of partial equilibrium models, an important contribution of the model is in illustrating how the direct impacts of forestry sector-specific policies are modified once the indirect effects arising from intersectoral linkages are accounted for. For example, partial equilibrium analysis predicts that stumpage price increases will reduce logging. However, the model shows that, while deforestation from logging will indeed decline, total deforestation nevertheless increases. The reason is that the contraction of the logging and forest industry sectors causes a shift of resources toward agriculture. As agriculture expands, deforestation increases.

The importance of these indirect effects is also demonstrated in the analysis of economywide policy changes, such as an increase in the wage rate. Because the role of intersectoral resource flows is incorporated in the CGE model, the effects of changes in wages are different from partial equilibrium results. If the wage of unskilled labor were increased due to, say, minimum wage legislation, the model predicts that deforestation could worsen instead of declining. Although logging declines due to increased direct costs, this is more than made up by the indirect effect of intersectoral flows since the industrial sector (where minimum wage legislation is more binding) is much more adversely affected by the higher labor costs. Labor and capital thus tend to flow to agriculture, leading to the conversion of forest land for farming.

Finally, both these last two examples suggest the importance of pursuing sectoral reforms in the context of growth. Without alternative employment opportunities, reducing logging activities will tend to direct labor and capital resources toward agriculture, industry and other sectors. Expansion of some of these sectors may lead to a second round of effects on forestry which could actually result in more deforestation.

Ghana[2]

In Ghana, socioeconomic and land-mapping data were combined to analyze the effects of ongoing trade liberalization and public employment reduction on agricultural productivity and land use in the country's western region. A key empirical result underlying the policy simulations is that the main source of supply response in agriculture is the expansion of cultivated area rather than agricultural intensification. It was estimated that biomass, measured in terms of the proportion of land under forest cover, is an important factor of production, contributing 15–20 percent of the value of agricultural output. This is close to the contribution of "conventional" factor inputs: 26 percent for land cultivated, 25 percent for labor, and 26 percent for capital. Since the share of agricultural output in national GDP is about 50 percent, this means that the contribution of biomass to national income is about 7.5 percent. Thus the stock of biomass is an important determinant not only of agricultural production but also of GDP.

In the agricultural system prevalent in the area, a large proportion of the land available in the village is reserved exclusively for the use of villagers. The system is consistent with shifting cultivation since the individual has exclusive rights on the land actually being cultivated, but once the land is left idle in fallow it can be reallocated by con-

---

[2]Researcher: Ramon Lopez.

sensus and consent of the village chief. Under these conditions, biomass is already being overexploited through a more than optimal level of land cultivated. Fallow periods appear to be too short, and the stock of the environmental resource is below socially optimum levels.

The study found that increasing agricultural prices or reducing wages cause an expansion in the cultivated area, with the direct effect of increasing output. For example, a 10 percent increase in land cultivated leads to a 2.7 percent increase in the direct output effect. However, such an increase in cultivated area leads to a reduction in fallowing, and total biomass declines by 14.5 percent. This, in turn, leads to a 2.5 percent loss in sustainable agricultural productivity. Thus, the net effect of expanding area cultivated (2.7 percent direct output effect less 2.5 percent biomass loss effect) is still positive but only 0.2 percent—many times smaller than the direct effect alone. In addition to policy changes, other factors contribute to expansion of cultivated area: large family size, availability of capital, and the presence of migrant populations in the area.

The results suggest that, in general, economywide price and wage policy reforms that do not include changes in land management practices will have limited impact on national income, once the existence of land quality effects is considered. This means that sustainable development efforts would be better served if such links between agricultural production and environmental degradation could be analyzed in the context of economywide reform programs.

Morocco[3]

The Morocco study focuses on the linkages between macroeconomic policies and

how the existing water allocation system has led to suboptimal and unsustainable patterns of water use. Specifically, low water charges (coupled with ineffective collection of these charges), have artificially promoted production of water intensive crops such as sugarcane. Thus, rural irrigation water accounts for 92 percent of the country's marketed water use. At the same time, irrigation charges cover less than 10 percent of the LRMC, and the corresponding figure for urban water tariffs is less than 50 percent. Given these policies, it is not surprising that a water deficit is projected for Morocco by the year 2020.

The study, however, goes beyond the traditional sectoral remedy of proposing an increase in water tariffs. It links sectoral policy reforms with ongoing macroeconomic adjustment policies, namely the complete removal of nominal trade tariffs, and analyzes the overall effects of both sets of reforms. As a consequence of the trade reforms, prices of sugar, cereals, oilseeds, meat and dairy products, among other things, would decline to world levels from their current protected levels. Further, a *simultaneous* introduction of trade and water pricing reforms would imply increased input prices and a decline in output prices. As in the Costa Rica case above, a CGE model is used to trace the impact of these reforms on output, consumption, imports, exports, and the use of factors of production (including water), by the different sectors in the economy.

To separate out the effects of the sectoral and macroeconomic reforms, the study considers three scenarios: water pricing reform only, trade reform only, and a combination of the two. In the first scenario the only policy change is a doubling in the price of rural irrigation water. Similarly, in the second scenario the only change is a complete removal of nominal tariffs (which in 1985 averaged 21 percent for the whole economy and 32 percent for agriculture). In

[3]Researchers: Ian Goldin and David Roland-Host.

the final scenario the two policy reforms are combined.

The results indicate that, other things being equal, reforming water prices alone reduces water use significantly—by 34 percent in rural areas and by 29 percent for the economy as a whole. This is as would be expected. This achievement of static efficiency, however, is acquired at a price: real GDP falls by about 0.65 percent, and incomes and real consumption of both rural and urban households decline by approximately 1 percent. In the second scenario, liberalization of trade only has the opposite effect: there is a marginal rise in real GDP, and household incomes and consumption post significant gains as import barriers are reduced, exports become more competitive, domestic purchasing power rises and resources are allocated more efficiently across the economy.

The two major drawbacks, however, are that elimination of tariffs leads to budgetary deficits and domestic water use increases substantially due to the expansionary effects of liberalization. In the final scenario, the expansionary effects of trade liberalization are retained, but reforming water prices still induces substantial reductions in agricultural (and economywide) water use. Moreover, this reduction in water consumption occurs against a backdrop of growth in real GDP unlike in the price reform only scenario.

Philippines[4]

The Philippines case study evaluates the policy determinants of long-term changes in rural poverty and unemployment that have motivated increasing lowland to upland migration. This process has led to the conversion of forest lands to unsustainable agriculture and has been identified as a key mechanism contributing to the deforestation

problem. The inability of the government to manage forest resources is an important direct cause of deforestation, but there is increasing recognition that economic policies, both sectoral and economywide, also significantly contribute to the problem. These policies take the form of direct sectoral interventions through agricultural taxation, price controls, subsidies, and marketing restrictions. They could also be indirect, working through exchange rate policies and industrial protection.

The study shows that in general these policies have tended to penalize lowland agriculture in favor of industrial sectors. On the one hand, this has resulted in the limited ability of the agricultural sector to productively employ a growing labor force. On the other hand, trade and exchange rate policies have made the industrial sector inefficient and increasingly difficult economic conditions during the late 1970s and early 1980s further reduced its lagging capacity to absorb surplus labor from the agricultural sector. The net result has been growing unemployment and worsening rural poverty, and these provide the "push" factors motivating migration to forest lands. Deforestation in the Philippines has exceeded 150,000 hectares per year of forest area for the last two decades. Conversion to agricultural land constitutes the largest form of land use change from forest land. Between 1980 and 1987, for example, the cultivated areas on land with 18–30 percent slope alone increased by more than 37,000 hectares annually.

The study evaluates government interventions for key crops to illustrate the role of commodity specific policies in altering the incentives for lowland compared with upland agriculture. Policies on rice production, which dominates lowland agriculture, have been governed more by the goal of maintaining low prices for consumers rather than assuring price incentives for producers. Corn and coconut production, which togeth-

[4]Researchers: Wilfrido Cruz, Herminia Francisco, and Gregory Amacher.

er make up the majority of agriculture in sloping lands, have also fared differently from government intervention. Corn cultivation has generally been encouraged while coconut, a more environmentally stable crop, has been excessively taxed. Corn, for example, has received favorable protection while the copra export prohibition and the coconut levy kept producer prices below world prices by more than 25 percent. The net effect of these policies has been to reduce the attractiveness of lowland compared with upland agriculture and to encourage upland farming households to shift from coconut farming to more environmentally demanding corn production.

In addition to commodity specific policies, trade and exchange rate policies have also played important roles and have been dominated by an urban consumer and industrial sector bias. The agricultural sector was implicitly taxed by an average of about 20 percent for most of the 1970s and early 1980s. Because the industrial sector did not provide an alternative source of growth, poverty in general has worsened and rural incomes in particular have suffered. An econometric model of migration from lowlands to forest lands indicates that the main mechanism through which these economic problems affect the environment is migration and the conversion of forest lands to unsustainable agriculture. Population pressure already evident in the 1970s worsened during the 1980s. The net upland migration rate grew from 3.4 to 9.4 percent between 1970–75 and 1978–80, and increased substantially to 14.5 percent between 1980 and 1985. Consequently, upland cropped area grew at annual rates exceeding 7 percent from 1971 to 1987. These results indicate that while forestry specific conservation programs are needed, economywide policy reforms are as important in arresting deforestation in the Philippines.

Poland[5]

The massive structural changes now occurring in Eastern Europe and China clearly present even greater analytical challenges in predicting the environmental impacts of economic reforms. The former centrally planned economies of Eastern Europe are burdened by the twin legacy of low energy prices and the absence of an incentive system that ensures efficient utilization of resources. This is exemplified in the Poland case study, which evaluates the relationship between economic reforms (including both price and institutional changes) and energy and air pollution issues. The assessment proposes that energy intensity and excessive pollution in Poland is due not only to the undervaluation of coal in the centralized price system but more importantly to the entire system of state ownership that encourages output maximization rather than cost minimization. This means that price responsiveness is blunted by the fact that financial losses are simply absorbed by the public budget, or passed on in the form of higher output prices.

In addition to the institutional constraints, Poland also explicitly pursued a macroeconomic strategy which emphasized rapid industrialization in general and the development of heavy industry in particular. Four energy-intensive industries—energy, metallurgy, chemicals and minerals—tended to dominate the sector. As a result, they were also the most polluting sectors in industry and made heavy demands on other natural resources, such as water. While an industrialization strategy based on heavy industry is common to most centrally planned economies, in the case of Poland, where coal is an abundant resource, it also led to excessive energy intensity.

---

[5]Researchers: Robin Bates, Shreekant Gupta, and Boguslaw Fiedor.

Finally, it was not only the types of economywide policies pursued in Poland which historically promoted high levels of energy use. Environmental policy was not used to offset adverse impacts of industrialization on the environment. To some extent, this was due to the lack of price responsiveness of state-owned enterprises, which limited the effectiveness of an otherwise sophisticated system of pollution taxes. In addition, environmental inspection and audit capabilities were weak and environmental statutes were not stringently enforced. For example, even by the end of the 1980s, only a third of plants emitting air pollutants had emission permits.

In 1990, Poland initiated an economic transformation program that led to the privatization of many enterprises. The program was beset by recession and the collapse of trading arrangements linked to the Council of Mutual Economic Assistance (CMEA). Furthermore, the process of privatization proved to be more complex and lengthy than initially expected. The government has therefore introduced an enterprise and bank restructuring program to assist in the restructuring of state-owned enterprises and in reducing their debt-servicing constraints.

Despite these changes, SOEs will continue to be major players in the Polish economy, at least in the short term. Of particular relevance is the decision by government to retain ownership in the energy, mining, steel and defense sectors in the medium term, and to decide on privatization on a case-by-case basis over the next three years. Thus, energy sector restructuring efforts have focused on creating the institutional and legal framework to facilitate competition and greater private sector participation in the future. Coupled with aggressive energy pricing reforms, this strategy appears to be making some headway. For example, a recent survey of large state-owned manufacturing concerns found that even without privatization, SOEs are already adjusting to the transformation program. In particular the survey found that all firms reduced their consumption of materials and energy per unit of sales.

While progress in economic reforms has already produced some results, the timing and speed of further change are matters of considerable uncertainty in Poland. The case study therefore analyzed a number of scenarios to quantify the possible impact of various economic reforms on the environment. Projections of energy generation and the associated emissions from three alternative models indicate clear environmental gains from restructuring combined with energy pricing reforms. Although there are improvements, the study also concluded that economic reforms by themselves will not be enough to meet the medium-term environmental goals set by government in 1991. Specifically, the simulations suggest that sulfur and particulate emissions will not be sufficiently reduced unless complementary environmental regulations are also adopted.

Sri Lanka[6]

World Bank work has traditionally addressed the problem of subsidies in key sectors such as energy and water, that result in inefficient use of these services. In Sri Lanka, the study approached the assessment of policy reforms and environmental concerns from two perspectives: by first investigating the environmental implications of energy sector pricing reforms and then by evaluating the effectiveness of alternative policy approaches in meeting specific environmental goals, such as reducing GHG emissions which is mandated by the World Climate Convention. The study focused on electricity price reforms as an example of a sectoral policy change with broad economic and environmental implications and on

[6]Researchers: Peter Meier, Mohan Munasinghe, and Tilak Siyambalapitiya.

evaluating the effectiveness of levying externality taxes on electricity compared with applying carbon taxes to meet GHG constraints.

The economic rationale for eliminating power subsidies or raising tariffs is documented in many studies, and covenants between the Bank and its borrowers often provide for tariff increases to generate sufficient revenue to meet self-financing or rate-of-return on equity targets. However, problems arise in evaluating the environmental consequences of such policies. For example, higher electricity prices, based on the LRMC of power generation, may be expected to encourage more efficient use of electricity. However, reduced consumption could also affect the least cost expansion path, such that the addition of more efficient generating units might be delayed, resulting in higher emissions.

The extent to which this effect would be offset by the lower generation requirement is an empirical question, which can only be answered by investigating specific cases. In projecting future electricity requirements in Sri Lanka, the study found that the efficiency effect of setting electricity prices to reflect LRMC dominates and there is a significant and unambiguously beneficial impact on the environment. The difference between tariffs based on average incremental cost of generation (as an approximation of LRMC) and one based merely on meeting financial covenants that require achieving a 10 percent return on equity is a 6 percent reduction of greenhouse gas emissions by the year 2010, and a 10 percent reduction in the health effects associated with human exposure to incremental ambient concentration of air pollutants. In addition, pricing reforms were found to have a more general impact than technical approaches to demand-side management (DSM), such as promoting the use of energy-saving fluorescent lights. DSM programs tend to be difficult to implement and limited in scope.

With respect to meeting GHG reduction goals, at present per capita carbon emissions in Sri Lanka (0.06 compared with 4.9 tons per capita in the United States) are extremely low, due to the dominance of hydropower sources and the low energy intensity of the industrial sector. However, beyond the year 2000, CO_2 emissions will rise very sharply as the generation mix moves toward fossil fuels. As generating capacity is increased, the study found that imposing carbon taxes on fuels has a more direct impact on greenhouse gas reductions than adding the equivalent externality cost (an environmental tax) to the electricity tariff. The reason is that the fuel tax gives more direct signals for implementing a power generation expansion path that reduces the use of "dirty" fuels such as coal.

Tunisia[7]

In Tunisia, the government's concern with increasing the country's self-sufficiency in livestock products and with the affordability of these products for its citizens has resulted in a web of pricing and subsidy interventions in the livestock sector. The environmental consequence of these measures, namely the degradation of Tunisia's rangelands, however, has rarely been a central consideration. A variety of subsidies has promoted the intensification of livestock production in certain parts of Tunisia, while in other regions government subsidies and policies have encouraged the maintenance of the national herd at levels beyond the carrying capacity of the country's rangelands.

Particularly during dry years, subsidized feed imports have provided a substitute for reduced grazing supplies, and have succeeded in averting the large declines in animal numbers often associated with droughts. This failure of livestock numbers

---

[7]Researchers: Zeinab Partow and Stephen Mink.

to respond to diminished feed availability in natural pastures, however, has contributed to significant environmental degradation of the Tunisian range. This has direct effects on livestock production, and longer-term, indirect implications for the entire agriculture sector. While important efforts at pasture improvement and reforestation are underway, the positive impact of these and other measures are often undermined by subsidy and pricing policies that fail to consider or respond to environmental signals.

Livestock policies have had different environmental impacts in the north, center and south regions of the country. Government subsidies for feed, irrigation and fertilizers have promoted intensification of livestock production and integration with cropping activities in the north. This has occurred to a lesser extent in the central part of the country, where sheep herds have increased without commensurate increase in feed production. Rangeland appears to be degrading, exacerbated by stabilization of herd sizes in drought years through the subsidized distribution of barley feed imports, and more generally through the mild protection of domestic mutton production. Following liberalization of mutton prices in the late 1970s it became profitable to increase use of feed concentrates for sheep production, but this has not been sufficient to alleviate the pressure on Tunisia's central rangelands.

In addition, government policy encouraged the conversion of marginal lands from pastures into cereals, mainly barley. Not only did this encourage land degradation through the removal of permanent cover, it also shifted some of the best pasture lands to marginal cereal production, further shrinking the rangeland resources available to a growing livestock herd. Thus while subsidies may have a beneficial effect when implemented in the north and perhaps in certain parts of central Tunisia, their impact

on rangelands in much of central and southern Tunisia has been negative. Failure of policies to distinguish between bioclimatic zones has thus contributed to the severe degradation of the country's range resources. The intention has been to protect herders in the southern and central regions from major losses and wide income fluctuations; this short-term objective has been accomplished, but no durable solution has been found to alleviate the herd pressure that is slowly degrading the capacity of rangeland to sustain herds and livestock income. In addition, subsidies on feed concentrates have reduced the incentives for forage production.

While government policy may have had a small measure of success in social terms, these benefits threaten to be short-lived if the environmental consequences of policies are not adequately considered. Income stabilization of small-scale herders will only be temporary if it is achieved through means that result in the degradation of the rangeland upon which the incomes ultimately depend. The long-term effects of environmental degradation will ultimately result in the permanent reduction of rangeland productivity and the consequent reduction of herd size and incomes from livestock. In addition, the impacts of increased desertification and soil erosion will find their way into the rest of the economy, affecting agricultural productivity and infrastructure (siltation of reservoirs through increased erosion). The challenge is to introduce less environmentally destructive means to achieve the social objectives.

Sweeping policy changes introduced gradually since the launching of structural adjustment reforms in 1986 will ultimately have an important impact on how livestock activities affect rangeland. These policy changes were primarily driven by budget constraints and market strategies, with environmental consequences rarely taken into account. The interaction of these policies makes it difficult to predict the magnitude of their impact on the various feed sources, and their introduction is still too recent for clear trends to be identifiable. It is probable that strengthening producer prices for beef will encourage growth in the cattle herd after years of stagnation. This growth will be concentrated initially in the north where feed resources are more abundant, but a critical issue will be whether the derived demand generated by cattle herd growth will help to maintain fodder and barley production in the face of reduced subsidies on fodder crop inputs such as irrigation water and fertilizer. In central Tunisia, the financial returns to sheep herding are likely to decline with subsidies being eliminated on feed concentrates, and some shift to beef production can be expected. The impact of such shift will depend on whether permanent cattle herds are maintained, or whether incentives encourage a focus on reproduction using seasonally available range feed resources for sale to fattening operations in the north.

Zimbabwe[8]

The study of the impacts of economic policies on wildlife in Zimbabwe, like the Tunisia case, illustrates the opportunity for economywide reforms that also have environmental benefits. The wildlife-based economic activities in this country, including eco-tourism, safaris, hunting, and specialized meat and hide production, constitute one of the fastest growing sectors of the economy. Wildlife-based tourism alone grew at the rate of 13 percent in 1991 and comprised 5 percent of GDP. The sector is also important from the environmental perspective. Wildlife-based activities, unlike cattle ranching, with which they compete for limited land resources, are better suited to

---

[8]Researchers: Kay Muir-Leresche, Jan Bojö, and Robert Cunliffe.

the country's semiarid climate and poor soils. The direct environmental advantage is that economically viable systems can be maintained with lower stocking rates than those associated with commercial cattle ranching and subsistence pastoral activities. Equally important is the indirect environmental benefit associated with wildlife management goals of conserving a natural habitat that appeals to visitors.

Thus, there has been much interest in wildlife development, with emphasis placed on its potential role as a more sustainable land use system than conventional agriculture in semiarid zones. Except for specially protected species, the 1975 Parks and Wildlife Act and its amendment for communal areas allowed wildlife utilization by the private sector to expand rapidly. Wildlife enterprises currently account for 15 percent of land use on commercial and communal lands. The large wildlife enterprises are found in arid areas where farmers concentrate on extensive game or mixed game and cattle ranching. Wildlife resources are generally not used for meat production, and most meat offtake is sold locally at prices well below beef prices. Nevertheless wildlife competes with beef production; not in terms of meat output but in terms of land use.

With respect to sectoral policies, government land policies have generally discouraged private sector involvement in wildlife activities since these are still perceived as "underutilizing" land and therefore invites future taxation or appropriation. Livestock marketing and price policies have also traditionally subsidized cattle ranching. Since 1985 subsidies directed to an inefficient parastatal marketing system have been the main cattle sector policy instrument.

Industrial promotion and exchange rate policies are two areas where there have been adverse effects on wildlife activities. Zimbabwe followed a strongly interventionist policy regime and the structural adjustment program initiated in 1990 has only marginally moved the economy toward liberalization. The problem is that Zimbabwe inherited a highly centralized and regulated economy at the time of independence. As recently as 1990, the government budget comprised 48 percent of GDP. This excessive public sector role in the economy crowded out private initiative and contributed to very low investment levels and productivity. Government policy tends to channel the limited private sector investment into the mining and manufacturing sectors, primarily through simplifying project assessment and approval procedures. In areas where wildlife resources are still abundant, the establishment of commercial schemes does not require major capital investment, and the sale of concessions for offtake or for viewing access can be used in initial development. However, even where wildlife activities may be socially beneficial, they will not be successful if government policies undermine their private profitability.

Foreign exchange controls, however, have played the more important role. For many years, the government's foreign exchange and trade policies have severely penalized this sector. The Zimbabwean dollar was overvalued by 50 to 80 percent from 1981 to 1990. This meant that export-oriented sectors were implicitly taxed, among them wildlife and nature tourism concerns. Foreign exchange earnings were diverted to other sectors, depressing incomes and investment in wildlife. In 1990, the government introduced an adjustment package, including measures aimed at boosting the level of exports. The currency was devalued by 25 percent, and more liberal access to foreign exchange was allowed. Although further progress needs to be made, these moves have contributed on both economic and ecological fronts. Exports increased; at the same time, the profitability of the wildlife sector increased, allowing an expansion of land allocated for wildlife.

Scope of Economywide Policy-Environment Linkages

While the case studies undertaken in this program focused on a particular environmental issue for each country, the various linkages between economywide policies and a range of environmental concerns presented above may be of relevance in other developing countries. Table 6–1 presents the scope the different findings from the case studies within a consolidated matrix.

In fact, land degradation, deforestation, industrial pollution, and energy inefficiency and water management problems could all occur in the same country. By identifying the possible linkages between policies and such environmental concerns, the examples drawn from these different country case studies may help guide future, more comprehensive studies of specific countries.

Table 6–1: Scope of Economywide Policy-Environment Linkages Discussed in Case Studies

Economic Policies and Other Measures	Erosion and Land Degradation	Deforestation	Pollution	Energy and Water Use
Macroeconomic Policies	Foreign exchange liberalization has increased profitability of ecotourism based on environmentally friendly wildlife industry (**Zimbabwe**) Agricultural price increases associated with liberalization lead to agricultural extensification and decline of fallowing and yields (**Ghana**)	Improved rural incomes and employment opportunities reduces lowland poverty and population pressure on fragile, open access forest lands (**Philippines**) High interest rates lead to increased deforestation; higher wage rates in industrial sector reduces employment and encourages expansion of both agriculture and deforestation (**Costa Rica**)	Financial sector reforms and privatization efforts impose harder budget constraints on state-owned enterprises, allowing higher coal prices to reduce pollution intensity (**Poland**)	Trade liberalization may promote economic expansion at cost of increased water use (**Morocco**)
Sectoral Policies	Livestock promotion policies have discouraged wildlife resource-based activities (**Zimbabwe**) Agricultural subsidies have led to overgrazing of arid and semiarid range lands (**Tunisia**)	Disadvantageous terms of trade of agriculture relative to industry penalized rural sector, aggravated migration into marginal forest lands (**Philippines**) Agricultural growth needed to reduce deforestation pressures (**Costa Rica**)	Low energy and fuel prices encouraged use and aggravated air pollution (**Poland, Sri Lanka**)	Marginal cost pricing of power promotes energy conservation (**Sri Lanka**) Underpricing of coal associated with excessive energy intensity of industry (**Poland**)
Explicit Environmental Policies		Increased stumpage valuation reduces logging but may lead to expansion of agriculture into forest areas (**Costa Rica**)	Taxation of carbon content in fuel use for energy leads to less use of "dirty" fuels such as coal (**Sri Lanka**)	Subsidies for industrial and agricultural water use undermines conservation (**Morocco**)

7

Policy Implications

EFFECTIVE DECISIONMAKING FOR SUSTAINABLE development
has been hindered by lack of knowledge about the complex
links between economywide policies and the environment.
From the economic side, the environmental implications of
macroeconomic policies and the adjustment process typically
inadequately explored, and from the environmental side,
national environmental action plans (NEAPs) rarely contain
careful economic analysis. As described below, several
practical steps to facilitate the integration of environmental
and economic decisionmaking emerge from the case studies.

Integrating Environmental Concerns into Economic Decisionmaking

The preceding discussion shows that the links between economywide policy reforms and the environment can be complex and usually require country-specific analysis. However, while impacts are often too diverse to be comprehensively traced with precision, many key economywide reforms have specific, identifiable, impacts on a much smaller subgroup of priority environmental problems. Some of these impacts may be intuitively obvious, and many of them, with some effort, may be traceable. Even modest progress in this regard is helpful because the proper recognition of the environmental benefits of economywide policies will clearly help build support for economic reforms. At the same time, broader recognition of the underlying economic and policy causes of environmental problems can enhance support for environmental initiatives—both in terms of environmental policies, as well as projects.

Positive or negative linkages may arise from relative price shifts—changes in the pattern of taxes, trade duties, real wages, exchange rates, and so on. For example, there are usually strong positive linkages between energy conservation and reforms in energy pricing. On the other hand, trade liberalization may encourage deforestation or overfishing in some cases. Where such negative linkages exist, the answer is not to delay stabilization or the adjustment program, but rather to devise specific measures, such as sensible forestry and fishing laws, to counteract the possible negative effects. In almost all cases the foregoing conclusions will be appropriate. However, it is conceivable that in rare cases involving more severe environmental degradation (especially where *ex ante* analysis has carefully prepared the ground), special care may be required to orchestrate the timing and se-

quencing of various economywide policies and complementary environmental measures, to minimize environmental damage.

The best approach to avoid environmental damage would thus be to identify, prioritize and analyze the most serious economic-environmental linkages, and devise specific complementary mitigating measures, when economywide reforms are contemplated. Where data and resource constraints preclude the accurate tracing of such links (*ex ante*), the preliminary screening and prioritization of environmental issues could be followed by establishing contingency plans and carefully monitoring these environmental problems, to deal with them if they worsen *ex post* (see the next section on Action Impact Matrix).

Action Impact Matrix: A Tool for Analysis

In the context of the foregoing discussion, economic and environmental analyses and policies may be used more effectively to achieve sustainable development goals, by linking and articulating these activities explicitly. Implementation of such an approach would be facilitated by constructing an Action Impact Matrix (AIM)—a simple example is shown in Table 7–1, although an actual AIM would be very much larger and more detailed.[1] Such a matrix helps to promote an integrated view, meshing economic decisions with priority environmental and social impacts.

The first column of Table 7–1 lists examples of the main development interventions (both policies and projects), while the first row indicates some of the main sustainable development issues. Thus the elements or cells in the matrix help to (a) explicitly identify the key linkages; (b) focus attention on valuation and other methods of analyzing the most important impacts; and (c) suggest

---

[1]Munasinghe 1993a.

action priorities. At the same time, the organization of the overall matrix facilitates the tracing of impacts, as well as the coherent articulation of the links between a range of development actions—that is, policies and projects.

A stepwise process, starting with readily available data, has been used effectively to develop the AIM in several country studies that have been initiated recently.[2] First, data from NEAPs, environmental assessments (EAs), and so forth may be organized into an environmental issues table that prioritizes these problems, provides quantitative or qualitative indicators of damage, and helps identify underlying economic causes. Second, the main economywide policies (current and intended) could be set out in a second table, together with a brief review of the basic economic issues that they address and potential environmental linkages. The information from these two tables is then combined to develop a preliminary action impact matrix. (For an example of this process, refer to Tables 7-2–7-4, which first present the environmental issues, then describe various economywide policy reforms, and finally combine these two building blocks to produce an illustrative Action Impact Matrix for Sri Lanka.)

One of the early objectives of the AIM-based process would be to help *in problem identification*—by preparing a preliminary matrix that identifies broad relationships, without necessarily being able to specify with any accuracy the magnitudes of the impacts or their relative priorities. For example, in Table 7–1, a currency devaluation may make timber exports more profitable and lead to deforestation of open access forest. The appropriate remedy might be to strengthen property rights or restrict access to the forest areas. A second example might involve increasing energy prices toward

marginal costs to improve energy efficiency and decrease pollution. Adding pollution taxes to marginal energy costs will further reduce pollution.

Increasing public sector accountability will reinforce favorable responses to these price incentives, by reducing the ability of inefficient firms to pass on cost increases to consumers or to transfer their losses to the government. In the same vein, a major hydroelectric project is shown in Table 7–1 as having two adverse impacts—inundation of forested areas and villages, as well as one positive impact—the replacement of thermal power generation (thereby reducing air pollution). A re-afforestation project coupled with adequate resettlement efforts may help address the negative impacts. The matrix-based approach therefore encourages the systematic articulation and coordination of policies and projects to achieve sustainable development goals. Based on readily available data, it would be possible to develop such an initial matrix for many countries.

This process may be developed further to assist in *analysis* and *remediation*. For example, more detailed analyses may be carried out for the subset of main economywide policies and environmental impact links identified in the cells of the preliminary matrix. This, in turn, would lead to a more refined final matrix, which would help to quantify impacts and formulate additional measures to enhance positive linkages and mitigate negative ones. The more detailed analyses which could help to determine the final matrix would depend on planning goals and available data and resources. They may range from the application of conventional sectoral economic analysis methods (appropriately modified in scope to incorporate environmental impacts), to fairly comprehensive system or multisector modeling efforts.

The former approach is used in many of the case studies mentioned above. The latter

---

[2] For example, Ghana and Sri Lanka. The process used in Sri Lanka is illustrated in Tables 7-2–7-4.

approach is illustrated by the **Costa Rica** and **Morocco** studies where computable general equilibrium models were constructed that includes both conventional economic, as well as environmental or resource variables. At the moment, data and analytical shortcomings are likely to preclude reliance upon general equilibrium or comprehensive system modeling approaches. Current efforts constitute a first step in this direction—their major contribution being to identify more precisely the information and data required for operational policy purposes, and test the strengths and limitations of a general equilibrium approach.

Thus far, the more successful attempts to value environmental impacts in the macroeconomic context, have been based on their effects on conventional economic output which are priced in the marketplace (supplemented sometimes with shadow pricing corrections). This approach may be linked up more easily with commonly used market measures of well-being like gross national product (GNP). For example, the new United Nations handbook for the System of National Accounts (SNA), includes a proposal to supplement the conventional SNA with a set of satellite accounts that reflect pollution damage and depreciation of natural resource stocks.[3]

Some environmentally and socially crucial impacts (for example, loss of biodiversity or human health hazards) may be as important in certain cases, and they may require extension or adaptation of conventional economic techniques. One step would be to improve environmental valuation by using a wider range of methods which employ both market and on-market information to indirectly estimate the economic value of environmental assets (for example, travel cost or contingent valuation methods). Such techniques have been used quite widely in

project-level applications in the industrial countries.[4] There is a growing body of case studies on the environmental valuation of project impacts in the developing countries.[5] However, considerable work is required to extend this experience to cover economywide impacts.

Other (noneconomic) indicators of environmental and social well-being (both micro and macro) also would be helpful in decisionmaking, especially in cases where economic valuation was difficult. Techniques such as multicriteria analysis (MCA) may be used to trade off among different economic, social and environmental indicators, as a supplement to conventional cost-benefit analysis. The **Sri Lanka** case study explores the MCA approach, in attempting to analyze economic-environmental, as well as environmental-environmental tradeoffs. The essential point is that even when environmental valuation is not possible, techniques exist that will help to better prioritize environmental and social impacts, thereby improving development actions.

Identifying Economic-Environmental Links

As shown above, the better integration of environmental issues in economywide policy analysis will help generate support for economic reforms. However, this can also improve the policy context for environmental initiatives. Implementation of projects that have environmental objectives or components has always been a problem. This stems from the fact that it may not be in the narrow self interest of the borrowing entity to adhere to loan conditions which are primarily of benefit to others in the country. At the national level, enforcement of standards

---

[3]United Nations Statistical Office (UNSO) 1993.

[4]For a recent review, see, for example, Freeman 1993.

[5]For a recent review, see, for example, Munasinghe 1993a.

and regulations often encounters severe institutional constraints. Part of the answer is to create conditions in which the interests of the party causing environmental damage coincide with the social good—integration of environmental concerns into sectoral and macroeconomic incentives is therefore required.

Overall, the studies discussed earlier suggest that economic techniques exist—and for most countries, so does natural resource information—to improve the way environmental issues are addressed by policies at the sector and macro levels. Although data problems remain, the studies illustrate the feasibility of carrying out better analyses of the environmental impact not only of projects, but also of economic policies—and in particular—adjustment operations. This will hasten the integration of the environment into the mainstream of economic policymaking. Where the environmental impact of the adjustment process is potentially adverse, such studies would form the basis for identifying measures to counteract these effects (both *ex ante* or *ex post*); where on the other hand they are likely to be positive, complementary measures might be devised to maximize such beneficial impacts.

This approach is consistent with and supports project environmental assessment (EA) procedures that are already in existence in most countries. While the function of the EA as a proactive instrument of project preparation and design is clearly understood in theory, more could be done to achieve this objective in practice. The "add-on" nature of environmental concerns, the lack of breadth in identifying relevant issues, the limited attention to alternatives and the weak mitigation plans in some projects show this to be the case. Clearly, the search for fundamental underlying causes of environmental degradation and the design of economic and other instruments at the country or sector level could substantially support the EA process at the project or investment level.

The lessons from the case studies are also relevant from the viewpoint of those with explicit environmental responsibilities, including preparation of National Environmental Action Plans (NEAPs). These documents have rarely responded adequately to the growing need for greater understanding of links between economic policies and the environment, and to date none have apparently conducted a systematic analysis of the economic policies underlying environmental degradation and, therefore, of the appropriate ways in which the environment should become part of countrywide economic planning.

In providing examples to those responsible for environmental management of the way in which economic policies may impact upon the environment, the evidence contained in this book demonstrates the kinds of opportunities available for achieving environmental objectives, not simply in a cost-effective manner, but indeed often in ways that impose no costs at all upon society. Such opportunities should receive systematic attention in country environmental action plans, which would then become much more operationally useful as inputs into decisionmaking at the macroeconomic or sector policy level.

In summary, the specific findings emerging from the case studies are presented below—grouped according to the principal ways in which economywide policies interact with the environment, highlighting how they might help in the design of better adjustment programs.

- Removal of major price distortions, promotion of market incentives, and relaxation of other constraints (which are among the main features of adjustment-related reforms), generally will contribute to both economic and environmental gains. Reforms which improve the efficiency of industrial or energy related activities could reduce both economic waste and environmental pollution. Similarly, improving land tenure rights and access to financial and social services not only yields economic gains but also promotes better environmental stewardship.

- Unintended adverse side effects may occur, however, when economywide reforms are undertaken while other neglected policy, market or institutional imperfections persist. Indeed the very success of the adjustment process in stimulating economic growth may place pressure on the environment due to inadequacies elsewhere in the economic, administrative, or legal system. Specific additional measures that remove such policy, market and institutional difficulties may not only be generally environmentally beneficial in their own right, but also critical complements to broaden economywide reforms. Typical examples include:

  Policy distortions: Export promotion and trade liberalization might encourage excessive extraction or harvesting of natural resources if the latter were underpriced or subsidized, for example, low stumpage fees for timber.

  Market failures: Economic expansion induced by successful adjustment may be associated with excessive environmental damage, for example, if external environmental effects of economic activities (such as pollution), are not adequately reflected in market prices.

  Institutional constraints: The environmental and economic benefits of economywide reforms could be negated by unaddressed institutional issues. These may include, for example, poor accountability of state-owned enterprises; inadequate land titling; weak financial intermediation; or inadequate capacity for monitoring and regulating the discharge of industrial waste.

- Measures aimed at restoring macroeconomic stability will generally yield environmental benefits, since instability undermines sustainable resource use. For example, stability encourages a longer-term view on the part of decisionmakers at all levels, while lower inflation rates lead to clearer pricing signals and better investment decisions by economic agents. These are essential prerequisites for encouraging environmentally sustainable activities.

- The stabilization process also may have unforeseen adverse short-term impacts on the environment, in some cases. For example, while general reductions in government spending are deemed appropriate, targeting these cutbacks would be desirable to avoid disproportionate penalties on environmental protection measures. Another important issue is the short-term impact of adjustment on poverty and unemployment, which may aggravate existing pressures on fragile and "open access" resources by the poor due to the lack of economic opportunities. In this case, appropriate measures designed to address the possible adverse social consequences of adjustment will be justified even further—on environmental grounds.

- Economywide policies will have additional longer-term effects on the environment through employment and income distribution changes. Several of the examples confirm one predictable conclusion—adjustment-induced changes generate new economic opportunities and sources of livelihood, thereby alleviating poverty and reducing pressures on the environment due to overexploitation of fragile resources by the unemployed.

However, while growth is an essential element of sustainable development, it will necessarily increase pressures on environmental resources. Increasing efficiency and reducing waste, as well as properly valuing resources, will help reshape the structure of growth and reduce undesirable environmental impacts.

Practical Implications

While the relationships between economywide policies and the environment are complex and involve many economic and noneconomic variables, immediate steps can be initiated by decisionmakers to improve understanding and to start to address some of these linkages. Proper recognition of the generally positive environmental consequences of economywide policy reforms could help to build additional support for such programs. At the same time, broader recognition of the underlying economic and policy causes of environmental problems can enhance support for environmental initiatives. The following are key practical steps that can be taken:

- *Problem Identification*: More systematic efforts are needed to *monitor environmental trends and anticipate emerging problems* when policy reform proposals are being prepared. The range of currently available environmental information should be analyzed to help identify the highest priority pre-existing or emerging environmental problems, and their sensitivity to policy measures. Recently initiated work on environmental indicators in the Bank would help supplement existing data.

- *Analysis*: Serious potential environmental impacts of proposed economywide reforms identified in the problem identification stage should be subjected to *careful environmental analysis*—to the extent that data and resources permit. Many of the techniques and examples presented in this chapter will be helpful in tracing the simpler and more obvious links between economywide policies and the environment.

- *Remedies*: Where potential adverse impacts of economywide reforms can be identified, *targeted complementary environmental policies or investments* should be implemented as soon as feasible—to mitigate predicted environmental damage, and enhance beneficial effects. Where linkages are difficult to trace *ex ante*, greater reliance will need to be placed on *preparing contingency plans* to be invoked *ex post* (see below).

- *Follow-up*: A *follow-up system for monitoring the impacts of economic reform programs on environmentally sensitive* areas (identified earlier) should be designed, and resources made available to address environmental problems that may arise during implementation.

The complementarity of economic and environmental measures for sustainable development should be used to mobilize more environmental support for economic reforms, and vice versa. However, the difficulties of analyzing the potential environmental impacts of proposed economywide reforms (*ex ante*), should not be underestimated. Linking specific causes with particular effects is especially problematic in countries where many conditions are simultaneously changing. Nevertheless, many direct linkages may be traced using existing methods. Since the better incorporation of environmental aspects into economic policymaking could result in substantial gains (particularly in the context of adjustment operations), more analytical work is needed to better understand the complex links involved. Due to the significance of social and institutional constraints to sustainable development, more attention should be paid also to the analysis of the social impacts of economywide reforms.

This book has shown how the analytical process may be strengthened, starting from fairly simple considerations. The various relationships identified here, although based on country-specific work, have been used to develop a general, framework based on the concept of the Action Impact Matrix (AIM), which more clearly identifies a country's environmental problems in relation to its program of economywide policy reforms and major projects. This stepwise approach focuses initially on the links among a relatively small subset of priority environmental concerns and a few key economic policy reforms. In subsequent stages, the analysis may be made much more comprehensive. In view of its potential contribution as a policy tool to link a wide range of environmental processes with macroeconomic and sector policies, it is recommended that governments give high priority to strengthening and refining the building blocks of the Action Impact Matrices applicable to their own country circumstances.

Table 7–1: Simple Example Action Impact Matrix (AIM)

ACTIVITY/POLICY	MAIN OBJECTIVE	MATRIX OF OTHER IMPACTS ON KEY SUSTAINABLE DEVELOPMENT ISSUES			
		Land degradation	Air pollution	Resettlement	Others
1. Macroeconomic and Sectoral Policies	Macroeconomic and Sectoral Improvements	Positive Impacts Due to Removal of Distortions Negative Impacts Mainly Due to Pre-existing Constraints			
● *Exchange Rate*	● Improve Trade Balance and Economic Growth	(-H) (deforest open-access areas)			
● *Energy Pricing*	● Improve Economic and Energy Use Efficiency		(+M) (improve energy efficiency)		
● *Others*					
2. Complementary Measures	Specific or Local Social and Environmental Improvements	Enhance Positive Impacts and Mitigate Negative Impacts (above) of Broader Macroeconomic and Sectoral Policies			
● *Market Based*	● Reverse Negative Impacts of Market Failures and Policy Distortions	(+H) (property rights)	(+(M)) (pollution tax)		
● *Non-Market Based*			(+M) (public sector accountability)		
3. Investment Projects	Improve Efficiency of Investments	Investment Decisions Made More Consistent with Broader Policy and Institutional Framework			
● *Project 1* (Hydro Dam)	● Use of Project Evaluation (Cost-Benefit Analysis, Environmental Assessments, Multi-Criteria Analysis, etc.)	(-H) (inundation)	(+M) (displace fossil fuel use)	(-M) (displace people)	
● *Project 2* (Re-afforest.)		(+H) (replant forest)			
● ●					
● *Project N*					

Note: A few examples of typical policies and projects as well as key environmental and social issues are shown. Some illustrative but qualitative impact assessments are also indicated: thus + and - signify beneficial and harmful impacts, while H and M indicate high and moderate severity. The AIM process focuses on the highest priority environmental issues and related social concerns.

Table 7-2: Example of Environmental Issues: Matrix Indicators and Causes of Selected Environmental Problems in Sri Lanka

Environmental areas of concern	Bio-physical indicators	Socioeconomic indicators	Underlying causes: economic policies, prices, and institutions
Soil erosion and degradation	Increasing pressure on land (land-man ratio has declined to 0.38 ha), as the economy continues to depend on land.	Productivity losses due to soil erosion estimated in the range of Rs. 613 to 4,283 million annually.	Land markets are very limited and the resource is severely underpriced. This leads to inefficient and distorted allocation decisions.
	Cultivation of marginal lands, particularly the shallow and lateritic soils of the wet zone, results in erosion and landslides. Forests have been removed from steep slopes for tobacco cultivation. Erosion rates in neglected tea lands (up to 30 percent of total area under tea) are as high as 40 tons/ha/yr, compared to an achievable rate of 0.3 tons/ha/yr.	Tea yields only 52–64 percent of yields in Indonesia, India, Malawi, and Kenya. Severe erosion has led to the Polgolla reservoir silting up to 45 percent of its capacity within only 12 years of operation, resulting in a loss of irrigated area, electricity generation, as well as greater flooding.	Land tenure system results in disincentives for long-term soil conservation measures. This includes poorly managed state-owned tea and rubber plantations. Subsidies for erosive crops (e.g., potatoes).
	In the dry zone where land is flat, erosion is not a severe problem. However, the longstanding practice of chena (shifting) cultivation is now practiced with greater intensity: very short fallow periods have replaced longer ones that made the system sustainable. As a result, soil is becoming infertile and about 1.2 million hectares of land (mostly in the dry zone) are now degraded.		In the case of gem mining, lack of environmental charges or rehabilitation deposits encourages small scale pit mining operations which do not reflect the social cost of these activities.
	Severe land degradation due to gem mining in specific areas (mostly in Ratnapura district).		
Deforestation and biodiversity loss	Decline in forest cover from 55 percent of total area (1950s) to 28 percent (1980s). NEAP estimates forest area in 1989 at 1.58 million ha (24 percent of total area), with closed canopy forest down to 20 percent. Deforestation rate is estimated to be 30,000–50,000 ha/yr.	Decline in sustainable timber yield due to deforestation is estimated at Rs. 300 million annually. The wood industry also has been forced to shift to lower quality wood. In addition, conversion forest land to chena, poorly managed plantations, or food crops results in soil erosion amounting to 5–10 percent of GNP.	Underpricing of timber (royalty only 10 percent of sales value) encourages maximization of current extraction at the expense of future harvesting. Poverty and unemployment leads to encroachment of forest lands (80 percent of which are state-owned, but de facto open access).
Urban and industrial pollution	Less than 20 percent of the population of Colombo Metropolitan Area (CMA) is served by sewers. Less than half of CMA's daily solid waste disposal of 1,200 tons reaches landfills.	Diseases associated with pollution and poor sanitation constitute the number one cause of morbidity and mortality in CMA.	Absence of user fees for municipal services results in financially weak municipalities that are dependent on govt. grants.
	Similar situation prevails in other urban areas as well. CMA is the only urban area with a (partial) sewer system.	Nationwide, the rate of intestinal infections more than doubled to 1,025 per 100,000 population between 1965–84.	Lack of effluent/emission charges implies that activities that generate them do not internalize the costs of these damages.

Table 7–2 (continued)

Environmental areas of concern	Bio-physical indicators	Socioeconomic indicators	Underlying causes: economic policies, prices, and institutions
Water pollution and water shortage	Water shortage in areas other than the western part of the wet zone.	A disproportionate share of public investment has been allocated to irrigation, particularly the Mahaweli project (public expenditure on this project alone accounted for 7 percent of GDP in 1982). However, the returns have not been commensurate.	Lack of effluent charges or enforceable standards.
	Sedimentation of reservoirs and canals in irrigated areas in the dry zone. Salinity and waterlogging in downstream lands also a growing problem.		Fertilizer subsidies result in overuse.
	Fertilizer residues from paddy cultivation contaminate surface and subsurface water. Poor fertilizer storage is one of the main causes of groundwater pollution.	Water use is inefficient (biased towards paddy cultivation). Large volume of water is unaccounted for (39 percent in Colombo) due to leaks, faulty meters and illegal connections.	Small size of holdings (1 ha) in Mahaweli, and the incentives provided by subsidies, trade policy and research and extension contribute to excessive concentration on (water intensive) paddy cultivation, as do land use and cropping restrictions. Area under high value added cash crops is limited in the Mahaweli, implying suboptimal use of irrigation water.
	Extensive water pollution in urban and industrial areas. Nearly 75 percent of Colombo's untreated sewage is discharged into the lower Kelani river. Water quality at the city's water intake at Ambatale often unfit for public water supply.	The irrigation infrastructure is deteriorating prematurely: funds allocated for operation and maintenance cover only 40 to 60 percent of the actual requirement.	National water tariff is below marginal cost and the collection system is relatively ineffective. Cross-subsidies (from low-cost to high-cost regions and from Greater Colombo to the rest of the country), discourage water conservation.
Marine and coastal resource degradation	One-third of the coastline (1,600 km) is subject to varying degrees of erosion. Average annual rates on the southwestern and western coasts range from 1 to 7 meters.	Potential sites for managed sand mining have largely disappeared.	Virtual open access to coral reefs and coastal fishery resources.
	Extensive sand and coral mining aggravate erosion. The latter is most severe along southwestern coast, where approx. 7,700 tons of coral and coral debris are collected annually along a 60 km stretch.	Coastal fisheries have declined.	Excessive reliance on legislation and laws for the protection of coastal resources. Mining of sea coral in the coastal zone (a punishable offence under the Coast Conservation Act), continues unabated. Though the demand for coral is a *derived demand* for construction, there has been no focus on economic incentives for reducing this (derived) demand by encouraging alternative construction materials.
	Sedimentation and runoff from rivers and agricultural lands, and inappropriate infrastructure also leads to coastal and marine degradation. There is a growing list of mangrove areas and lagoons that have been seriously damaged by pollution.	Coastal tourism potential in sites such as Hikkaduwa and Bentota is threatened by fecal pollution of beaches and coastal waters. (About 85 percent of tourist revenue comes from facilities in coastal areas. About 75 percent of graded hotels and over 80 percent of hotel rooms are located along the coast. Thus, tourism is threatened by (as well as a cause of) marine and coastal resource degradation.	In terms of agrochemical runoff, fertilizer and pesticide subsidies are a major cause of overuse.
Energy shortage	Fuelwood accounts for 70 percent of energy consumption, and is used for cooking by 94 percent of households. Fuelwood shortage forecast in the dry zone by 1995 and for the entire country by 2000.	Industry is relatively energy intensive, and households generally do not practice energy conservation. Thermal efficiency of traditional stoves is 10–15 percent.	Electricity tariffs are low. Even after a 30.5 percent increase in 1993, average tariff (6 cents/Kwh) is approx. two-thirds of the long run marginal cost (LRMC). Households consumers are cross-subsidized (some pay only 15 percent of LRMC). Uneconomic rural electrification
	No domestic petroleum. All large hydropower resources (50 percent of hydro potential) already tapped.		

Table 7–3: *Current Economic Conditions and Proposed Reforms in Sri Lanka*

Macro policies	*Current situation/policy regime*	*Ongoing/proposed reforms*
Government Budget	Deficit has crowded out the private sector and driving up real interest rates. It was 11.6 percent of GDP in 1991. However, in 1992, a 1 percent reduction in current expenditure and a sharp drop in capital expenditure reduced deficit to 7.5 percent, well below the target of 8.6 percent. It went up to 8.1 percent of GDP in 1993.	Reduce overall deficit (excluding official grants) to 6.5 percent of GDP in 1994, through improved revenue performance, consolidation of current expenditures, and rationalization of the public investment program. Reduce deficit to ≤6 percent in the long run.
(i) Govt. Expenditures	Misallocated: large, unviable investment programs; inadequate maintenance expenditures; excess spending on civil service salaries, defense and debt servicing.	Limit large village-level public works programs; administrative reform, including civil service reform; $600 million Airbus purchase by Air Lanka should be reconsidered.
(ii) Public Enterprises	Losing money: losses at 8 largest ones accounted for half of the deficit in 1991; 2 state-owned banks with ⅔ of total assets of banking sector are insolvent.	Half of small/medium enterprises already privatized or divested. Complete the privatization of small/medium enterprises, start with large ones (Air Lanka, sugar factories, cement companies, tea plantations)—also see *Industry* below. However, no sign that hard budgets will be imposed on the ones that remain state-owned (e.g., Ceylon Electricity Board (CEB), Sri Lanka Railways (SLR) and Ceylon Petroleum Corporation (CPC)). CEB's tariffs are to be increased in 1994 & 1995 due to IDA pressure. SLR has been made into an autonomous corporation and an IDA-assisted restructuring program is under way. (*May Day package announced by the President actually lowers electricity tariffs!*)
Sectoral policies		
(iii) Tax Policy	Substantial reliance on indirect taxation (83 percent); arbitrariness (proliferation of tax holidays, ad hoc tax concessions).	A VAT was planned for 1994, but has been postponed by a year to April 1995. Progress in computerizing returns continues to be slow. Corporate income tax reduced to 45 percent; elimination of export taxes; simplification of turnover tax (rate bands reduced from 10 to 3).
•*Infrastructure/Energy*	Transport, telecommunications, electricity generation are heavily concentrated in the public sector; backlog of necessary rehabilitation and maintenance works; inadequate cost recovery; regulatory framework inhibits private sector entry.	Sri Lanka Telecom Dept. is now a public corporation. In addition, there is now a limited role for private services in this sector. Sri Lanka Railways has been converted from a govt. department to an independent authority.
	Ceylon Electricity Board (CEB) and Sri Lanka Railways (SLR) require tariff and fare hikes urgently. In former tariffs are well below long-run marginal cost (LRMC). Level and structure of petroleum prices out of line with border price relatives; public import monopoly of petroleum products.	No increase in long-awaited tariff and fare revisions for CEB and SLR, respectively; no indication that tariffs in the infrastructure sector in general will be increased towards long run marginal cost (LRMC). BOO/BOOT schemes are being actively pursued in the power sector.
	The massive Mahaweli project has been going on since 1970 (almost complete now) to provide irrigation and electricity. It is the govt's largest investment project: over 43 billion rupees had been spent by 1987 and the total expenditure was then anticipated at 60 billion rupees (Sri Lanka's GDP in 1987 was 200 billion rupees).	Private sector entry allowed in petroleum sector (e.g., blending plant and blending services privatized and divestiture of retail stations is ongoing). Inadequate operation and maintenance (O&M) is already causing premature deterioration of the infrastructure. It is now necessary to focus on maintenance and rehabilitation rather than further investment. Studies by International Irrigation Management Institute (IIMI) indicate there is no economic justification to increase irrigated area such as through the Kalu Ganga project.

Table 7–3 (continued)

Sectoral policies	Current situation/policy regime	Ongoing/proposed reforms
•Industry/Mining	Manufacturing most dynamic sector in the economy (grew at 9 percent in 1992). Private sector grew at 20 percent and its performance overshadows the sluggish public sector. Foreign investment remains strong. This should enable the economy to grow and diversify its industrial and export base. Garment industry highly successful (partly due to import quotas in the EC and the United States). The government set up 200 rural clothing factories by the end of 1992 to promote job growth in rural areas and reduce the current concentration around Colombo—however, many may not be economically viable; also this is the only major nonagricultural manufactured export. A worrying development is that the United States has imposed a countervailing duty of 3.06 percent on all garment imports from Sri Lanka w.e.f. October 1993. This is a major blow since the United States accounts for 65 percent of all garment exports.	Privatization continues, and 23 state enterprises had been privatized by the end of 1992. However, plans to privatize Air Lanka and the two banks have not taken off. Following protests from local gem miners and environmentalists, the government in January, banned mechanized gem mining in all rivers and stream beds in Sri Lanka. (Possible environmental impacts: destruction of river fauna, lowering of surrounding water table, collapse of river banks leading to flooding in heavy rains.) Comprehensive new mining regulations introduced under an Act in 1992. All current licensed and unlicensed operations involved in exploration, mining, processing, trading or export of minerals must acquire new licenses under the act. The act does not cover gems and hydrocarbons.
•Agriculture	Sluggish growth and narrow export base due to (i) excessive govt intervention in pricing and trade; (ii) public expenditure excessively oriented toward self-sufficiency in food (free land and water inputs); (iii) poor O&M of existing irrigation infrastructure. Dominant crops are paddy, tea, rubber and coconut. Most of rubber and tea are exported. Tea: Output almost back to normal in 1993 after the drought-affected slump of 1992 (also due to privatization of plantation management). World demand is high and prices are firm. There is an urgent need to modernize tea industry and increase output of CTC tea (Western markets) as compared to orthodox teas. (In 1993 CTC tea accounted for only 3.4 percent of total output; the rest was orthodox tea—this could be a big problem in the future.) Tea growers also hampered by high interest rates. Another major problem is advanced age of tea bushes—in 1987 average age was approx 60 years. Only 15 percent of the area under tea had been replanted with HYVs. Low replanting in 1960s and 1970s because high export taxes + low tea prices = low profits; also there was a risk of nationalization. Rubber: A large number of plantations suffer from old age and neglect; output and area have been declining since the 1980s. Coconut: Like tea and rubber, suffers from inadequate replanting. Large proportion of trees old and past optimum productivity levels. Output is on a declining trend due to recurring droughts and withdrawal of fertilizer subsidies.	Insufficient political will to implement meaningful reform, especially to relax legislated cropping and land use restrictions and to remove nontariff barriers. Export crop taxation, however, being phased out; rationalization of sugar industry (including privatization of factories); rice, wheat and flour markets partially deregulated; tea and rubber plantations contracted out to private management companies (see below); Mahaweli restructuring plan under preparation. The govt. is offering cash subsidies per hectare to tea smallholders as well as rebates on fertilizers (environmental dilemma here—fertilizer subsidies bad for the environment, but required to increase production); tea marketing system to be reformed; regulations on tea growing relaxed—growers do not have to register tea holdings with the Tea Commissioner or obtain permits for planting and replanting, establishing nurseries or factories, or selling tea locally. There is a proposal to conduct the Colombo tea auction in dollars rather than rupees (enabling planters to borrow working capital in foreign currency, at much lower interest rates). Smallholders, who produce the bulk of the coconut output have not taken advantage of several subsidy schemes that the government has offered to encourage coconut production.
•Forests	Continuing deforestation and degradation of forests through illicit felling and encroachments which are periodically "regularized"; lax implementation of statutes for limiting felling; lot of good plans on the books but not implemented. The Forestry Master Plan (1987) is the blueprint for this sector for the next two decades. (∃ two types of forests: dry zone and all other.) While a large reforestation program has been implemented, essential follow-up silvicultural operations are frequently neglected.	The Master Plan envisages clearing all 1.3 million ha of dry zone forest (except 0.5 million ha set aside for national parks). The remaining forests are in the wet, intermediate and montane zones (278,000 ha). Of these 159,000 ha (57 percent) will be protected and the rest selectively cut. The Plan also recommends reintroduction of the cooperative reforestation scheme (a highly successful program for raising industrial wood plantations in the dry zone). A five-year program to improve the forests' condition and management started in 1990.

Table 7-4: Sri Lanka Action Impact Matrix

Economywide policy reform goals/ instruments	Urban and industrial pollution	Forest and biodiversity protection	Agricultural land conversion and degradation	Energy generation and conservation	Water resources depletion and degradation	Coastal resource degradation
Sectoral/intersectoral price and institutional reforms:						
• resource access rights and tenure	[+] property rights allowing community-based management of coastal areas and coral reefs could increase the incentives to reduce industrial and agricultural pollution	[+] decentralization and social forestry-type institutional support will reduce open-access exploitation of forest and wildlife resources	[+] tenurial security will promote land investment and improve land management (note: in some cases, privatization may be externally imposed on lands that are communally managed, leading to a breakdown of traditional management systems)			[+] introduction of community rights over fishing and mangrove resources would encourage better resource management
• price and subsidy reforms			[+] removal of subsidies will encourage more efficient/reduced use of agricultural chemicals	[+] improving energy prices will promote more efficient energy generation and use	[+] introducing higher industrial and irrigation water fees will encourage efficiency in water supply and use	
Privatization:						
• improve efficiency in use of resources (e.g., with financial reforms and hard budget constraints)	[+] reduce waste in resource-based manufacturing		[+] increase efficiency of tea plantations, leading to better land management (note: in lands that are governed by traditional communal systems, privatization may be associated with negative effects, as discussed under institutional reforms below)	[+] improve efficiency of generating plants; with pricing reforms (see below), it will also reduce energy intensity among industrial users	[+] promote more efficient provision of urban and industrial water supply	
• promote private investment	[+] private investments tend to introduce less polluting technology	[+] alienating land for plantations or allowing sufficiently long-term leases could promote plantation development	[+] may increase investment in land improvement	[+] new plants tend to be energy efficient	[-] together with price increases, this may reduce access to water by the poor	

Table 7–4 (continued)

Economywide policy reform goals/instruments	Pollution: industrial, urban, and coastal (including coral reefs)	Forest and biodiversity protection	Agricultural land conversion and degradation	Energy generation and conservation	Water resources depletion and degradation	Coastal resource degradation
Government deficit reduction:						
• cut expenditures, reduce subsidies	[-] social and environmental programs like urban pollution abatement (e.g., MEIP) are often the first to be cut; poorer communities often at risk	[-] protection efforts may be reduced especially in forestry (e.g., Forest Dept. budget constraints)	[-] reduced agricultural extension programs, increasing problem of chena cultivation, soil erosion	[+/] reduced energy subsidies also controls wasteful energy use, but may reduce access for the poor	[+/-] reduced subsidies will discourage wasteful water use but poor communities may have reduced access to safe supplies	[-] coastal/coral reef protection efforts may further decline (e.g., CEA, NARA budget constraints)
• introduce resource rent taxation and user charges		[+] reduce pressures on use of forests and protected areas and raise funds to improve community self-management or government protection services	[+] taxation of idle or neglected lands will encourage land improvement		[+] encourage more efficient use of water sources	[+] promote more efficient use of coastal resources
• introduce environmental taxes and fees (in contrast to above instruments, these are taxes on environmental externalities)	[+] taxes or charges on emissions or effluents will increase incentives for abatement; may also reduce land degradation from mining	[+] reforestation deposits could encourage sustainable logging		[+] introduce incentives to reduce emissions or effluents in energy generation	[+] tailings or discharge fee will reduce water degradation problems	[+] charges or penalties would discourage coral reef and mangrove degradation

Table 7–4 (continued)

Economywide policy reform goals/instruments	Pollution: industrial, urban, and coastal (including coral reefs)	Forest and biodiversity protection	Agricultural land conversion and degradation	Energy generation and conservation	Water resources depletion and degradation	Coastal resource degradation
Trade promotion:						
• export promotion and foreign exchange liberalization		[-] export stimulus may increase timber cutting; depending on land tenure and accountability this may worsen deforestation	[+/-] both crop output and input prices will be affected if they are tradables; better land management is encouraged by higher crop prices if tenure is secure (see tenure issue below)	[-] outward-oriented growth will increase energy generation needs		
• reduce tariffs and other trade barriers	[-/+] industrial openness is associated with new and more efficient technologies, but absolute pollution levels may increase with rapid sectoral growth		[+/-] may initially affect industrial output and employment as inefficient firms fail to compete with imports; long-run improvements in resource allocation should increase employment and income, reducing pressures for marginal resource exploitation			
Industrial promotion:						
• reduce special industry programs and investment subsidies	[+] special government industrial projects tend to favor industries (especially parastatals) that are often pollution prone; thus, reducing direct government programs will help change structure of industrial output		[+] increased industrial employment may reduce pressures on marginal lands			[+] tourism promotion could generate new jobs, reducing pressure on coral mining and fishery overexploitation

Alfsen, K. H. 1991. *Use of Macroeconomic Models in Analysis of Environmental Problems in Norway and Consequences for Environmental Statistics.* Discussion Paper, Oslo, Norway: Central Bureau of Statistics.

Alfsen, K. H., S. Glomsrod, and D. Hanson. 1987. "Direct and Indirect Effects of Reducing SO_2 Emissions: Experimental Calculations on the MSG-4E Model." Discussion Paper No. 20. Central Bureau of Statistics, Oslo, Norway.

Anderson, Dennis. 1980. "Environmental Policy and the Public Revenue in Developing Countries." Environment Department Working Paper No. 36, World Bank, Washington, D.C.

Anderson, J. R., and D. J. Thampapillai. 1991. "Soil Conservation in Developing Countries: A Review of causes and Remedies. 1991-07." *Quarterly Journal of International Agriculture (Germany)* 30:210–23, July–September.

Anderson, K., and R. Blackhurst. 1992. *The Greening of World Trade Issues.* New York: Harvester Wheatsheaf.

Aoyama, S., et al. 1994. *Japan's Experience in Urban Environmental Management.* Metropolitan Environmental Improvement Program. Washington, D.C.: World Bank.

Armstrong-Wright, A. 1992. *Urban Transit Systems: Guidelines for Examining Options.* Technical Paper No. 52. Urban Transport Series. Washington, D.C.: World Bank.

Barbier, E. 1988. "The Economics of Farm-Level Adoption of Soil Conservation Measures in the Uplands of Java." Environment Department Working Paper No. 11. World Bank, Washington, D.C., October.

Barbier, E. 1991. *The Role of Smallholder Producer Prices in Land Degradation—The Case of Malawi.* Paper presented at the European Association of Environmental and Resource Economics Annual Meeting, Stockholm, June.

Barbier, E., B. Aylward, J. Burgess, and J. Bishop. 1991. "Environmental Effects of Trade in the Forestry Sector." Paper prepared for the Joint Session of Trade and Environment Experts, OECD Paris, London Environmental Economics Centre, International Institute for Environment and Development, London, October.

Barghouti, Shawki, and Guy Le Moigne. 1991. "Irrigation and the Environmental Challenge." *Finance and Development* 28:32–33, June.

Bates, R., J. Cofala, and M. Toman. 1994. *Alternative Policies for the Control of Air Pollution in Poland.* World Bank Environment Paper No. 7. Washington, D.C.: World Bank.

Baumol, W., and W. Oates. 1988. *The Theory of Environmental Policy*, 2nd edition. New York: Cambridge University Press.

Bergman, L. 1989. "Energy, Environment and Economic Growth in Sweden: A CGE Modeling Approach." International Institute for Applied Systems Analysis (IIASA), Laxenburg, Austria.

Bernstein, J. 1993. *Alternative Approaches to Pollution Control and Waste Management: Regulatory and Economic Instruments.* Urban Management Program Discussion Paper. World Bank, Washington, D.C.

Bhatia, Ramesh, and Malin Falkenmark. 1992. "Water Resource Policies and the Urban Poor: Innovative Approaches and Policy Imperatives." Background Paper for the International Conference on Water and the Environment: Development Issues for the 21st Century, convened in Dublin, Ireland, January.

Binswanger, H. 1989. "Brazilian Policies that Encourage Deforestation in the Amazon." Environment Working Paper No. 16. World Bank, Environment Department, Washington, D.C.

Birdsall, N., and D. Wheeler. 1992. "Trade Policy and Industrial Pollution in Latin America: Where are the Pollution Havens?" In P. Low (ed.), *International Trade and the Environment*. World Bank Discussion Papers No. 159. Washington, D.C.: World Bank.

Blejer, M., and I. Guerrero. 1990. "The Impact of Macroeconomic Policies on Income Distribution: An Empirical Study of the Philippines." *Review of Economics and Statistics* LXXII (3):414–23.

Brandon, C., and R. Ramankutty. 1993. "Towards an Environmental Strategy for Asia." World Bank, Asia Technical Department, Washington, D.C.

Braun, J. von, and E. Kennedy. 1986. *Commercialization of Subsistence Agriculture: Income and Nutritional Effects in Developing Countries*. Washington, D.C.: International Food Policy Research Institute.

Burgess, J. C. 1991. "Environmental Effects of Trade on Endangered Species and Biodiversity." Paper prepared for the Joint Session of Trade and Environment Experts, OECD Paris, London Environmental Economics Centre, International Institute for Environment and Development, London, November.

Capistrano, A., and C. Kiker. 1990. "Global Economic Influences on Tropical Closed Broadleaved Forest Depletion, 1967–1985." Paper presented at the International Society for Ecological Economics Conference, World Bank, Washington, D.C., May.

Clark, C. 1976. *Mathematical Bioeconomics*. Baltimore, Md.: Johns Hopkins University Press.

Cleaver, K., and G. Schreiber. 1991. "The Population, Environment and Agriculture Nexus in Sub-Saharan Africa." Africa Region Technical Paper. Washington, D.C.: World Bank.

Coase, R. 1960. "The Problem of Social Cost." *Journal of Law and Economics.* October.

Cooper-Weil, D., et al. 1990. *The Impact of Development Policies on Health.* Geneva: World Health Organization.

Cornia, G., R. Jolly, and F. Stewart (eds.). 1987. *Adjustment with a Human Face, Volume l, Protecting the Vulnerable and Promoting Growth.* Oxford, U.K.: Clarendon Press, and New York: Oxford University Press.

Cromwell, C., and J. Winpenny. 1991. *Has Economic Reform Harmed the Environment? A Review of Structural Adjustment in Malawi.* London: Overseas Development Institute.

Cruz, W. 1986. "Open Access and Fishery Over-Exploitation in San Miguel Bay, Philippines." In *Common Property Resource Management.* Washington, D.C.: National Academy of Sciences.

Cruz, W., and M. Delos Angeles. 1988. "Forest and Upland Resource Management: A Policy Framework." *Journal of Philippine Development* 15(1):1–14.

Cruz, W., and C. Gibbs. 1990. "Resource Policy Reform in the Context of Population Pressure: The Philippines and Nepal." *American Journal of Agricultural Economics* 72(5).

Cruz, M. C., C. Meyer, R. Repetto, and R. Woodward. 1992. *Population Growth, Poverty, and Environmental Stress: Frontier Migration in the Philippines and Costa Rica.* Washington, D.C.:World Resources Institute.

Cruz, W., and R. Repetto. 1992. *The Environmental Effects of Stabilization and Structural Adjustment Programs: The Philippines Case.* Washington, D.C.: World Resources Institute.

Daly, H., and J. Cobb. 1989. *For the Common Good.* Boston: Beacon Press.

Dasgupta, P., and K.-G. Mäler. 1990. "The Environment and Emerging Development Issues." *Proceedings of the World Bank Annual Conference on Development Economics*, Supplement to *The World Bank Economic Review* and *The World Bank Research Observer*.

Devarajan, S. 1990. "Can Computable General Equilibrium Models Shed Light on the Environmental Problems of Developing Countries." Paper prepared for WIDER Conference on the Environment and Emerging Development Issues, Helsinki, September.

Dixon, J., et al. 1986. *Economic Analysis of the Environmental Impacts of Development Projects.* Manila: Asian Development Bank.

Dobson, P., R. Bernier, and A. Sarris. 1990. *Macroeconomic Adjustment and the Poor—The Case of Madagascar.* Cornell Food and Nutrition Policy Program, Monograph 9. Ithaca, N.Y.

Economic Commission for Latin America and the Caribbean (ECLAC). 1989. *Crisis, External Debt, Macroeconomic Policies and Their Relation to the Environment in Latin America and the Caribbean.* Paper prepared for the Meeting of High-Level Government Experts on Regional Co-operation in Environmental Matters in Latin America and the Caribbean, United Nations Environmental Programme, Brasilia.

Eskeland, G. 1992. "Attacking Air Pollution in Mexico City." *Finance and Development* 29(4):28–30.

Eskeland, G. 1993. "A Presumptive Tax on Gasoline: Analysis of an Air Pollution Program for Mexico City." Policy Research Working Paper No. WPS 1076. World Bank, Country Economics Department, Washington D.C.

Eskeland, G., and E. Jimenez. 1991. "Choosing Policy Instruments for Pollution Control: A Review." Policy Research Working Paper No. 624. World Bank, Country Economics Department, Washington, D.C.

Feder, G., T. Onchan, Y. Chalamwong, and C. Hongladarom. 1988. *Land Policies and Farm Productivity in Thailand.* Baltimore: Johns Hopkins University Press.

Fontaine, J. M., and A. Sindzingre.1991. "Macro-economic Linkages: Structural Adjustment and Fertilizer Policy in Sub-Saharan Africa." Technical Papers (International) No. 49. Paris: Organisation for Economic Co-operation and Development Centre.

Freeman, A. III, 1993. *The Measurement of Environmental and Resource Values: Themes and Methods.* Washington, D.C.: Resources for the Future.

Glickman, J., and D. Teter. 1991. *Debt, Structural Adjustment, and Deforestation: Examining the Links—A Policy Exercise for the Sierra Club.* Cambridge, Massachusetts: Harvard University.

Goldin, I., and D. Roland-Host. 1994. "Economic Policies for Sustainable Resource Use in Morocco." Paper prepared for the Joint Meeting on Sustainable Economic Development: Domestic and International Policy, sponsored by the OECD Development Center and

Center for Economic Policy Research (CEPR), Paris, May 24–25, 1993.

Grossman, G., and A. Krueger. 1991. "Environmental Impacts of a North American Free Trade Agreement." Discussion Papers in Economics. Princeton University, New Jersey, November.

Hamilton, K., and J. O'Connor. 1994. "Genuine Saving and the Financing of Investment." World Bank, Environment Department, Washington, D.C.

Hansen, S. 1988. "Debt for Nature Swaps: Overview and Discussion of Key Issues." Environment Working Paper No. 1. World Bank, Washington, D.C.

————. 1990. "Macroeconomic Policies and Sustainable Development in the Third World." *Journal of International Development* 2(4).

————. 1990. "Macroeconomic Policies: Influence on the Environment." In J. T. Winpenny (ed.), *Development Research: The Environmental Challenge*. London: Overseas Development Institute.

Harold, C., and C. Runge. 1993. "GATT and the Environment: Policy Research Needs." Staff Paper P93-5. University of Minnesota, Department of Agricultural and Applied Economics, St. Paul, Minnesota, January.

Hayami, Y., and Ruttan, V. 1971. *Agricultural Development in an International Perspective*. Baltimore: Johns Hopkins University Press.

Heggie, I. 1989. "Transport and the Environment: World Bank Policies and Experience." Infrastructure and Urban Development Department Reprints. World Bank, Washington D.C.

Holmberg, J. 1991. *Poverty, Environment and Development—Proposals for Action*. Stockholm: Swedish International Development Authority.

Hu, T., and J. J. Warford. 1994. "Economic Transition and Sustainable Agriculture in China." Project Report. World Bank, Pollution and Environmental Economics Division, Washington D.C.

Hueting, R. 1980. *New Scarcity and Economic Growth: More Welfare Through Less Production*. Amsterdam: North-Holland Publishing Company.

Hufschmidt, M., et al., 1983. *Natural Systems and Development: An Economic Valuation Guide*, Baltimore: Johns Hopkins University Press.

Hughes, G. 1992. "Cleaning Up Eastern Europe." *Finance and Development* 29(3).

Huq, M., and D. Wheeler. 1993. "Pollution Reduction Without Formal Regulation: Evidence from Bangladesh." Environment Department Divisional Paper No. 1993-39. World Bank, Washington, D.C., January.

Hyde, W., D. Newman, and R. Sedjo. 1991. *Forest Economics and Policy Analysis: An Overview*. World Bank Discussion Papers No. 134. Washington, D.C.: World Bank.

International Development Association. 1992. *IDA's Policies, Operations, and Finance in the Second Year of the Ninth Replenishment (FY92)*. Washington, D.C.

Johnson, D. Gale. 1973. *World Agriculture in Disarray*. London: Macmillan Press Ltd.

Kahn, J., and J. McDonald. 1991. "Third World Debt and Tropical Deforestation." Prepared by the Oak Ridge National Laboratory, Oak Ridge, Tennessee, for the U.S. Department of Energy.

Kneese, A. 1964. *The Economics of Regional Water Quality Management*. Baltimore, Md.: Johns Hopkins University Press.

Kosmo, M. 1989. "Commercial Energy Subsidies in Developing Countries." *Energy Policy* 17:244–253.

Krueger, A., M. Schiff, and A. Valdes. 1991. *The Political Economy of Agricultural Pricing Policies*. Washington, D.C.: World Bank.

Larson, B., and D. Bromley. 1991. "Natural Resource Prices, Export Policies, and Deforestation: The Case of Sudan." *World Development*, October.

Lele, U., and S. Stone. 1989. "Population Pressure, the Environment and Agricultural Intensification: Variations on the Boserup Hypothesis." MADIA Discussion Paper No. 4. World Bank, Washington, D.C.

Leonard, H. 1988. *Pollution and the Struggle for the World Product: Multinational Corporations, Environment, and International Comparative Advantage*. New York: Cambridge University Press.

Leonard, H. (ed.). 1989. *Environment and the Poor: Development Strategies for a Common Agenda*. Rutgers University, N.J.: Transaction Books.

Lindberg, K. 1991. "Policies for Maximizing Nature Tourism's Ecological and Economic Benefits." International Conservation Financing Project Working Paper, World Resources Institute, Washington, D.C.

Lockwood, B., and K. Ruddle. 1976. *Small-Scale Fisheries Development: Social Science Contribution*. Proceedings of a planning meeting held at the East-West Center Food Institute, September 6–11.

London Economics. 1991. *Economic Criteria in Assessing Global Warming Objectives*. London: London Economics.

Lopez, R. 1991. "Trade Policy, Economic Growth and Environmental Degradation." Symposium on International Trade and the Environment, World Bank, Washington, D.C.

———.1992. "Resource Degradation, Community Controls and Agricultural Productivity in Tropical Areas." Unpublished paper, University of Maryland, College Park, Md.

Low, P. (ed.). 1992. *International Trade and the Environment*. World Bank Discussion Papers No. 159. Washington, D.C.: World Bank.

Lutz, E. 1992. "Integration of Environmental Concerns into Agricultural Policies of Industrial and Developing Countries." *World Development* 20(2):241–53.

——— (ed.). 1993. *Toward Improved Accounting for the Environment*. Washington, D.C.: World Bank.

Lutz, E., and M. Munasinghe. 1991. "Accounting for the Environment." *Finance and Development* 28(1):19–21.

Lutz, E., et al. 1993. "Interdisciplinary Fact-Finding on Current Deforestation in Costa Rica." Environment Working Paper No. 61. World Bank, Environment Department, Washington, D.C., September.

Mahar, D. 1988. "Government Policies and Deforestation in Brazil's Amazon Region." Environment Working Paper No. 7. World Bank, Environment Department, Washington, D.C., June.

Manne, A., and R. Richels. 1990. "CO2 Emissions Limits: An Economic Analysis for the USA." *Energy Journal* 11.

Margulis, S. 1994. "The Use of Economic Instruments in Environmental Policies: The Experiences of Brazil, Mexico, Chile and Argentina." In *Applying Economic Instruments to Environmental Policies in OECD and Dynamic Non-Member Economies*. OECD, Paris.

Meier, G. (ed.). 1983. *Pricing Policy for Development Management*. Baltimore, Md.: Johns Hopkins University Press.

Meier, P., and M. Munasinghe. 1993. "Incorporating Environmental Costs into Power Development Planning: A Case Study of Sri Lanka." In M. Munasinghe (ed.), *Environmental Economics and*

Natural Resource Management in Developing Countries. Washington, D.C.: World Bank-Committee of International Development Institutions on the Environment (CIDIE).

Middleton, R., R. Saunders, and J. J. Warford. 1978. "The Costs and Benefits of Water Metering." *Journal of the Institution of Water Engineers and Scientists*, March.

Mink, S. 1993. "Poverty and the Environment." *Finance and Development* 30(4):8–10.

Munasinghe, M. 1990. *Electric Power Economics*. London: Butterworths Press.

———. 1992. *Water Supply and Environmental Management*. Boulder, Colorado: Westview Press.

———. 1993a. "The Economist's Approach to Sustainable Development." *Finance and Development* 30(4):16–19.

———. 1993b. *Environmental Economics and Sustainable Development*. Environment Paper No. 3. Washington, D.C.: World Bank, July.

Munasinghe, M., W. Cruz, and J. Warford. 1993. "Are Economywide Policies Good for the Environment?" *Finance and Development* 30(3):40–43.

Munasinghe, M., and K. King. 1991. "Issues and Options in Implementing the Montreal Protocol in Developing Countries." Environment Working Paper No. 49. Washington, D.C.: World Bank.

Munasinghe, M., and J. Warford. 1982. *Electricity Pricing—Theory and Case Studies*. Baltimore, Md.: Johns Hopkins University Press.

Miranda, K., and T. Muzondo. 1991. "Public Policy and the Environment." *Finance and Development* 28(2):25–27.

Nordhaus, W. 1991. "The Cost of Slowing Climate Change: A Survey." *Energy Journal* 12.

O'Connor, D. 1993. "The Use of Economic Instruments in Environmental Management—The East Asian Experience." Paper prepared for the Informal Workshop on the Use of Economic Instruments in Environmental Policies, OECD, Paris, October.

Opschoor, J., and H. Vos. 1988. *The Application of Economic Instruments for Environmental Protection in OECD Member Countries*. Paris: OECD.

Organisation for Economic Co-operation and Development (OECD). 1975. *The Polluter Pays Principle*. Paris: Organization for Economic Cooperation and Development.

———. 1991. *Environmental Policy: How to Apply Economic Instruments*. Paris: OECD.

———. 1993. "The Role of Economic Instruments in OECD member Countries." Paper prepared by OECD Secretariat for the Informal Workshop on the Use of Economic Instruments in Environmental Policies, OECD, Paris, October.

Page, T. 1977. *Conservation and Economic Efficiency*. Baltimore, Md.: Johns Hopkins University Press.

Panayotou, T., and C. Sussangkarn. 1991. "The Debt Crisis, Structural Adjustment and the Environment: The Case of Thailand." Paper prepared for the World Wildlife Fund Project on the Impact of Macroeconomic Adjustment on the Environment, October.

Pearce, D. 1986. *Cost Benefit Analysis*. London: Macmillan.

Pearce, D., and K. Turner. 1990. *Economics of Natural Resources and the Environment*. Baltimore, Md.: Johns Hopkins University Press.

Pearce, D., and J. J. Warford. 1993. *World Without End: Economics, Environment and Sustainable Development*. New York: Oxford University Press.

Pearce, D., et al. 1993, *Blueprint 3: Measuring Sustainable Development*. London: Earthscan Publications.

Perrings, C. 1993. "Pastoral Strategies in Sub-Saharan Africa: The Economic and Ecological Sustainability of Dryland Range Management." Environment Working Paper No. 57. World Bank, Environment Department, Washington, D.C., February.

Perrings, C., H. Opschoor, J. Arntzen, A. Gilbert, and D. Pearce. 1988. *Economics for Sustainable Development— Botswana: A Case Study*. Gaborone: Ministry of Finance and Development Planning, July.

Phantumvanit, D., and T. Panayotou. 1990. *Industrialization and Environmental Quality: Paying the Price*. Bangkok: Thailand Development Research Institute.

Reed, D. (ed.). 1992. *Structural Adjustment and the Environment*. Boulder, Colorado: Westview Press.

Reisen, H., and A. Van Trotsenburg. 1988. *Developing Country Debt: The Budgetary and Transfer Problem*. Paris: OECD.

Repetto, R. 1985. *Paying the Price: Pesticide Subsidies in Developing Countries*. Washington, D.C.: World Resources Institute.

Repetto, R. 1986. *Skimming the Water: Rent-seeking and the Performance of Public Irrigation Systems*. Washington, D.C.: World Resources Institute.

Repetto, R. 1989. "Economic Incentives for Sustainable Production." In G. Schramm and J. Warford (eds.), *Environmental Management and Economic Development*. Baltimore, Md.: Johns Hopkins University Press.

Repetto, R., and M. Gillis. 1988. *Public Policies and the Misuse of Forest Resources*. Cambridge, U.K.: Cambridge University Press.

Repetto, R., et al. 1989. *Wasting Assets: Natural Resources in the National Income Accounts*. Washington, D.C.: World Resources Institute.

Robinson, S. 1990. "Pollution, Market Failure, and Optimal Policy in an Economywide Framework." Working Paper No. 559. University of California at Berkeley, Department of Agricultural and Resource Economics, Berkeley, Cal.

Sasmojo, S., and M. Tasrif. 1991. "CO_2 Emissions Reduction by Deregulation and Fossil Fuel Taxation, A Case Study of Indonesia." *Energy Policy*, December.

Saunders, R., and S. Gandhi. 1993. *A World Bank Policy Paper: Energy Efficiency and Conservation in the Developing World*. Washington, D.C.: World Bank.

Saunders, R., J. J. Warford, and P. Mann. 1977. "Alternative Concepts of Marginal Cost for Public Utility Pricing." Staff Working Paper. World Bank, Washington D.C.

Scarsborough, E. 1991. "The Environmental Effects of Macroeconomic and Sectoral Policy in Chile and Peru." Unpublished discussion paper, Latin America and Caribbean Department, Environment Division, World Bank, Washington, D.C., July.

Schneider, R., et al. 1993. *Sustainability, Yield Loss and Imediatismo: Choice of Techniques at the Frontier*. Latin America and the Caribbean Environment Division (LATEN) Dissemination Note No. 1. World Bank, Washington, D.C., April.

———. 1993. *Land Abandonment, Property Rights, and Agricultural Sustainability in the Amazon*. LATEN

Dissemination Note No. 3, World Bank, Washington, D.C., April.

Schuh, G. 1974. "The Exchange Rate and U.S. Agriculture." *American Journal of Agricultural Economics* 56:1.

Sebastian, I., and A. Alicbusan. 1986. "Sustainable Development: Issues in Adjustment Lending Policies." Environment Department Divisional Paper No. 1989-6. World Bank, Washington, D.C., October.

Shilling, J. 1992. "Reflections on Debt and the Environment." *Finance and Development* 29(2):28–30.

Solorzano, R., et al. 1991. *Accounts Overdue: Natural Resource Depreciation in Costa Rica*, Washington, D.C.: World Resources Institute; and San Jose, Costa Rica: Tropical Science Center.

Southgate, D., and D. Pearce. 1988. "Agricultural Colonization and Environmental Degradation in Frontier Developing Economies." Environment Working Paper No. 9. World Bank, Environment Department, Washington, D.C., October.

Steer, A., and E. Lutz. 1993. "Measuring Environmentally Sustainable Development." *Finance and Development* 30(4):20–23.

Stryker, J., et al. 1989. "Linkages Between Policy Reform and Natural Resource Management in Sub-Saharan Africa." Unpublished paper. Fletcher School, Tufts University, and Associates for International Resources and Development, June.

Torfs, M. 1991. "Effects of the IMF Structural Adjustment Programs on Social Sectors of Third World Countries." Unpublished discussion paper. Friends of the Earth, Washington, D.C.

Ten Kate, A. 1993. "Industrial Development and the Environment in Mexico." Policy Research Working Paper No. 1125. World Bank, Washington, D.C., April.

Tietenberg, T. 1985. *Emissions Trading*. Baltimore, Md.: Johns Hopkins University Press. United Nations Secretariat, 1992. *Revised System of National Accounts, Chapter XXI, Satellite Analysis and Accounts*. New York: United Nations Development Programme.

United Nations Statistical Office (UNSO). 1993. *System of National Accounts 1993*. New York.

von Braun, J., and E. Kennedy. 1986. *Commercialization of Subsistence Agriculture: Income and Nutritional Effects in Developing Countries*. Washington, D.C.: International Food Policy Research Institute.

Warford, J. J. 1995. *Health Economics (Environment, Health, and Sustainable Development: The Role of Economic Instruments and Policies)*. Geneva: World Health Organization Task Force in Health Economics.

Warford, J. J., and D. Julius. 1977. "The Multiple Objectives of Water Rate Policy in Less Developed Countries." *Water Supply and Management* 1:335–42.

Warford, J. J., A. Schwab, W. Cruz, and S. Hansen. 1994. "The Evolution of Environmental Concerns in Adjustment Lending: A Review." Environment Department Working Paper No. 65. World Bank, Washington, D.C.

Wheeler, D., and M. Huq. 1993. "Pollution Reduction without Formal Regulation: Evidence from Bangladesh." Environment Department Divisional Paper No. 1993-39. Washington, D.C.: World Bank.

Wheeler, D., and P. Martin. 1993. "National Economic Policy and Industrial Pollution: The Case of Indonesia, 1975–89." Paper presented at the Workshop on

Economywide Policies and the Environment, World Bank, Washington D.C.

World Bank. 1980. *World Development Report 1980*. New York: Oxford University Press.

———. 1986. "World Bank Lending Conditionality: A Review of Cost Recovery in Irrigation Projects." Report No. 6283. World Bank, Operations and Evaluation Department (OED), Washington, D.C.

———. 1987. "Environment, Growth, and Development." Development Committee Paper No. 14. World Bank, Washington, D.C.

———. 1989a. *Philippines: Environment and Natural Resource Management Study*, Washington, D.C.: World Bank.

———. 1989b. *Sub-Saharan Africa: From Crisis to Sustainable Growth*. Washington, D.C.: World Bank.

———. 1989c. "World Bank Support of the Environment—A Progress Report." Development Committee Paper No. 22. World Bank, Washington, D.C., September.

———. 1990. "Towards the Development of an Environmental Action Plan for Nigeria." Report No. 9002-UNI. World Bank, Washington, D.C.

———. 1991a. *Environmental Assessment Sourcebook*. World Bank, Environment Department, Washington, D.C.

———. 1991b. "Environmental Assessment Operational Directive." World Bank, Washington, D.C., October.

———. 1991c. "The Forest Sector." A World Bank Policy Paper. World Bank, Washington D.C.

———. 1992a. *Adjustment Lending Policy*. OD 8.60. World Bank, Washington, D.C.

———. 1992b. An Agricultural Growth and Rural Environment Strategy for the Coastal and Central African Francophone Countries. Report No.

9592-AFR. Washington, D.C.: World Bank.

———. 1992c. *China Environmental Strategy Paper*. Report No. 9669-CHA. World Bank, Washington, D.C.

———. 1992d. *Economic Report on Environmental Policy—Malawi*. Report No. 9888-MAI. World Bank, Washington, D.C.

———. 1992e. "Operational Directive on Environmental Action Plans." World Bank, Washington, D.C.

———. 1992f. *Indonesia: A Strategy for Infrastructure Development*. Report No. 9672-IND. World Bank, Washington D.C.

———. 1992g. *Poverty Reduction Handbook*. Washington, D.C.: World Bank.

———. 1992h. *Water Supply and Sanitation Projects, The Bank's Experience: 1967–1989*, Report No. 10789, OED. World Bank, Washington, D.C.

———. 1992i. "The Welfare Consequences of Selling Public Enterprises: Case Studies from Malaysia, Mexico, Chile, and the U.K." Country Economics Department Working Paper. Washington, D.C.: World Bank.

———. 1992j. *World Bank Structural and Sectoral Adjustment Operations: The Second OED Review*. World Bank, Operations and Evaluation Department, Washington, D.C.

———. 1992k. *World Development Report 1992: Development and the Environment*. New York: Oxford University Press.

———. 1993. *The World Bank and the Environment, Fiscal 1993*. Washington, D.C.: World Bank.

———. 1993a. *Democratic Republic of Sao Tome and Principe: Country Economic Memorandum and Key Elements of an Environmental Strategy*. Report No.

10383-STP. World Bank, Washington, D.C.

———. 1993b. *Energy Efficiency and Conservation in the Developing World.* A World Bank Policy Paper. World Bank, Washington, D.C.

———. 1993c. *Environmental Action Program for Central and Eastern Europe.* Report No. 10603-ECA. World Bank, Washington, D.C.

———. 1993d. *Indonesia Environment and Development: Challenges for the Future.* Report No. 12083-IND. World Bank, Washington, D.C.

———. 1993e. *Jamaica Economic Issues for Environmental Management.* Report No. 11239-JM. World Bank, Washington, D.C.

———. 1993f. *Malaysia: Managing the Costs of Urban Pollution.* Report No. 11764-MA. World Bank, Washington, D.C.

———. 1993g. *Peru: Privatization Adjustment Loan.* Report No. P-5929-PE. World Bank, Washington, D.C.

———. 1993h. *Setting Environmental Priorities in Central and Eastern Europe.* Report No. 11099. World Bank, Washington, D.C.

———. 1993i. *Water Resources Management.* A World Bank Policy Paper. World Bank, Washington, D.C.

———. 1993j. *The World Bank and the Environment: Fiscal 1993.* World Bank, Washington, D.C.

———. 1993k. *The World Bank's Role in the Electric Power Sector.* A World Bank Policy Paper. World Bank, Washington, D.C.

———. 1994a. *Adjustment in Africa: Reforms, Results and the Road Ahead.* A World Bank Policy Research Report. World Bank, Washington, D.C.

———. 1994b. *Sierra Leone: Initial Assessment of Environmental Problems.* Report No. 11920-SL. World Bank, Washington, D.C.

———. 1994c. *Thailand: Mitigating Pollution and Congestion Impacts in a High-Growth Economy.* Report No. 11770-TH. World Bank, Washington, D.C.

World Commission on Environment and Development (WCED). 1987. *Our Common Future.* Oxford, U.K.: Oxford University Press.

World Resources Institute. 1989. *Natural Endowments: Financing Resource Conservation for Development.* Washington, D.C., September.

Yepes, G. 1992. "Water Supply and Sanitation Sector." *Infrastructure Maintenance in LAC: The Costs of Neglect and Options for Improvement, Volume 3.* Report No. 17. World Bank, Latin America and the Caribbean (LAC) Technical Dept., Regional Studies Program, Washington, D.C., p. 9.

AFC	average financial cost
AIC	average incremental cost
AIM	Action Impact Matrix
BAT	best available technology
CAC	command-and-control (measures)
CEB	Ceylon Electricity Board
CEE	Central and Eastern Europe
CES	constant elasticity of substitution
CET	constant elasticity of transformation
CFC	chlorofluorocarbon
CFL	compact fluorescent lighting
CGC	*Caisse de Compensation General*
CGE	computable general equilibrium (model)
CIDIE	Committee of International Development Institutions on the Environment
c.i.f.	cost, insurance, and freight
CITES	Convention on the International Trade in Endangered Species of Flora and Fauna
CMEA	Council of Mutual Economic Assistance
CSC	Cold Storage Commission (Zimbabwe)
DC	district council (Zimbabwe)
DHE	district heating enterprises
DNPWLM	Department of National Parks and Wildlife Management (Zimbabwe)
DSM	demand-side management
EA	environmental assessment
EAP	environmental action plan
EC	European Community
ECLAC	U.N. Economic Commission for Latin America and the Caribbean
EER	energy-efficient refrigerator
EPRI	Electric Power Research Institute
ERS	export retention scheme
ESAP	Economic Standard Adjustment Program
ETP	Economic Transformation Program
FGD	flue gas desulfurization
f.o.b.	free on board
FY	fiscal year
GATT	General Agreement on Tariffs and Trade
GDP	gross domestic product
GEF	Global Environment Facility
GHG	greenhouse gas
GJ	gigajoule
GNP	gross national product
GTZ	German Technical Assistance Agency (*Gesellschaft für Technische Zusammenarbeit*)

IAST	Institute of Agrarian Studies
IPCC	Intergovernmental Panel on Climate Change
LP	linear programming
LRMC	long-run marginal cost
LSS	Living Standards Survey
MADIA	Managing Agricultural Development in Africa
MEC	marginal external cost
MIT	Polish Ministry of Industry and Trade
MOC	marginal opportunity cost
MPC	marginal private cost
MUC	marginal user cost
NAFTA	North American Free Trade Agreement
NEAP	national environmental action plan
NEPP	National Environmental Policy of Poland
NGO	nongovernmental organization
NPR	nominal protection rate
NPV	net present value
NWMT	Nyaminyami Wildlife Management Trust (Zimbabwe)
OECD	Organisation for Economic Co-operation and Development
OED	Operations Evaluation Department of the World Bank
OLS	ordinary least squares
OS	oil steam-electric
p.a.	per annum
PFBC	pressurized fluidized bed combustion
PM	particulate matter
PPGC	Polish Power Grid Company
PPP	Purchasing Power Parity
SAM	social accounting matrix
SNA	System of National Accounts
SOCB	state-owned commercial bank
SOE	state-owned enterprise
SRMC	short-run marginal cost
T&D	transmission and distribution
TJ	terajoule
UN	United Nations
UNSO	United Nations Statistical Office
VIDCO	village development committee
VIM	vehicle inspection and maintenance (program)
WADCO	ward development committee
WCED	World Commission on Environment and Development
WHO	World Health Organization
WPA	Wildlife Producers Association
ZIC	Zimbabwe Investment Centre